To HOLLY,
my wife, mother of my two sons and two daughters,
sky-diver, white-water rafter, huntress, re-enactor, trekker,
and my canoe partner on the "voyages" of life.

"Wolves and hawks mate forever."

❧ Contents

❦ List of Illustrations and Photographs

❧ FOREWORD

By Steve Blanchard

*F*ebruary 10, 2002, I sat down to enjoy my Sunday newspaper and discovered on the inside front page, to my surprise, a half-page article dedicated to Robert Rogers and his 1757 "Rules of Ranging." While no serious student of history can ignore the role of Rogers in the French and Indian War I have to admit that my French/Irish/Scots/Native American heritage was more than a little vexed by his notoriety at the expense of his more than worthy adversaries. It should be noted however that history is indeed written by the winners and the roles played by those on the French side often are downplayed or even ignored. The book that you now hold in your hand, to paraphrase Paul Harvey, tells "the rest of the story."

Leading By Example: Partisan Fighters and Leaders of New France, Vol. 1 is Bob Bearor's third book and, in my opinion, the best of the three. *The Battle on Snowshoes* (Heritage Books, Inc., 1997) and *French and Indian War Battlesites: A Controversy* (Heritage Books, Inc., 2000) both deal with battles, locations and tactics more than with individuals but *Leading By Example* concentrates on the people involved in the battle for control of North America. These brave men who, from the outset stood little chance of ultimately defeating the might of Great Britain, fought as courageously for their homes and country as any on the other side, but sadly have been forgotten by history …until now! You are about to meet some of these forgotten heroes and I can honestly say after having read *Leading By Example* my view of the French and Indian War has been altered by the addition of the other side!

It was my privilege to be a part of the planning committee for "The Death of Lord Howe Reenactment" held in Ticonderoga, New York, on June 22, 2001. The scope of that reenactment was huge, stretching from Fort William Henry in the south to Ticonderoga in the north and involved hundreds of people...before even the first spectator arrived. The man who coordinated it all, held it all together and sprouted many a gray hair was Bob Bearor. Over the twelve months it took to make this reenactment a reality I had contact with Bob in committee meetings, working lunches at the Hot Biscuit Diner, coffee at the Hancock House and more telephone calls than either one of us cares to remember, I saw him work through countless issues and decisions, each one handled in a thoughtful and courteous manner. I may not have always agreed with him but he never failed to listen and in my opinion that says a lot about his character. As a student of history I highly recommend his latest effort to anyone with an interest in the French and Indian War. This book, the result of hours of research, is clearly, as stated in all his books, Bob's opinion and you the reader are free to agree or disagree based on your interpretation of the facts presented. In other words from the very beginning you are encouraged to form your own opinion. *Leading By Example* however is not another dry history book citing fact after fact and destined for the shelf of a library but rather a book for the common man and I think you will find it well worth your time and worthy of a permanent place in your home history library.

Finally, the day of "The Death of Lord Howe Reenactment" was overcast and humid and the French forces, led by Bob Bearor, were marching wearily toward

Ticonderoga having spent the night on Mt. Pélée (Rogers Rock). While marching down Baldwin Road towards the final safety inspection point at Ticonderoga Elementary School they met elements of the press who asked if they were the British forces. I think the answer given by Holly Bearor, Bob's wife, sums up *Leading By Example*:

"No, we're the good guys…we're the French!"

Sit back and get comfortable because you are about to be introduced to the good guys!

Stephen E. Blanchard
Former Assistant Director
Ticonderoga Historical Society

PARTISAN (Pär´ ti zan)
  1. Strong supporter of a party or cause
  2. Guerilla. Taking part in irregular fighting.

LEADER
  1. Person who leads.
  2. Person followed by others.

*Robert Rogers spent most of the Seven Years' War leading
Ranger units that were supposed to replace the Indian allies
that the British lacked. He tried indefatigably to perfect the
Rangers' skills in woodlands warfare, yet never entirely
succeeded in doing so; twice he and his men suffered terribly
(and he himself nearly died) at the hands of the French
Marines and Indians whose expertise was of a markedly
higher order.*

— Fred Anderson, *Crucible of War*

❧ INTRODUCTION

W hen writing this book, it was not my purpose or intention to make it a detailed, in-depth study of partisan leaders of New France. It could not be done fairly or thoroughly enough. Indeed, these men whom I have picked for the chapters in this book were only a very few of the many great leaders and fighters who shaped and molded the colony of New France. Also, it should be noted that, I have only highlighted certain dramatic events in each of their lives.

The serious researcher and "source hound" will have already known of and further examined the lives of these men meticulously. It is not for these scholars that I have written this book.

Instead, I wish to reach out to the ordinary readers and lovers of history; to show them that history is not just dates, times, and places; that these men are not just dusty old paintings, statues, or stories. They were real, alive, flesh and blood; they knew the feelings of victory and defeat, love and hate, war and peace, hardship, pain, and euphoria. They were not much different than we are; they just lived in a different time and place.

Also, there is another purpose to this book. It is to show and share with the reader another side; a side whose greatest loss might not have been to the English in the conquest and surrender of Canada in 1763, but in the loss of their fame and glory to today's readers.

Because we live today in the United States of America, English is our predominant language, and our lifestyles, then and now, are a result of the influence of our English predecessors. The history books that we read today about the French and Indian wars were either penned by English writers or Americans whose views were ingrained and formed by their English counterparts.

Case in point: Since my first book, *The Battle on Snowshoes,* was published in 1997, my wife, Holly, and I have appeared in eight states plus Canada, presenting our slide show at over 100 events at various forts, museums, libraries and historical societies. While speaking at these gatherings, I was amazed and saddened to learn that, while most of the people had heard of Robert Rogers and his Rangers, hardly any of them had heard of or were familiar with Langy (Langis), the famous French partisan who had beaten Rogers soundly three times.

Movies, books, and articles have been written about Robert Rogers *ad nauseum.* His epic march and raid to St. Francis — and indeed it was epic — is held up as the ultimate in hardship, success, and suffering, and is made to make Rogers look like the baddest S.O.B. in the valley. Really?

If one digs just a little deeper, he can find several examples of French partisan heroics that match and even surpass those of the brash, young Rogers.

Take Saint-Luc de La Corne, a veteran partisan who was shipwrecked off the coast of Nova Scotia in the dead of winter. En route from Canada to France, the ship *Auguste* was dashed to pieces on the rugged coastline, and the sixty-year-old La Corne managed to save himself but could not save the more than 100 others who perished in the icy waters of the North Atlantic, including his sons, nephews and brothers. Even after that harrowing experience, this tough old partisan led the six other survivors back through the snows to Quebec, more than 1500 miles away!

Then there was the partisan leader Gaspard-Joseph Chaussegros de Léry, who, when ordered to attack the English forts at the Oneida carry, left Fort La Présentation in March of 1756 (*not* one of the milder months like September and October, when Rogers made his St. Francis Raid), led a force of 362 men on snowshoes over a 260-mile round trip, and attacked a manned English fort that had been alarmed (*not* a village full of women and children). There, de Léry and his men fought a pitched battle, put the garrison to the sword, blew the fort up, and returned with a loss of only three men.

Canadians should not ever be ashamed of the loss of Quebec or Canada in the French and Indian War. Author René Chartrand titled one of his books, *Ticonderoga 1758: Montcalm's Victory Against All Odds*, and that pretty much tells it all. Canada, outnumbered 25 to 1, had really no chance against the overwhelming power of the British Empire. The fact that they fought and held on for seven years is a tribute to their fighting men.

In reenacting, we seek to honor those who made history. The largest numbers of reenactors in the United States choose to portray the men of both sides of our civil war. At ANY reenactment or encampment, both the North and South, Yankees and Confederates, are proud of their history — and both exhibit the same *esprit de corps*! Neither side seeks to change or rewrite history, only to pay honor to the men that they choose to represent.

I cannot recommend strongly enough the reading of such epics as *Montcalm and Wolfe* by Francis Parkman, *Wilderness Empire* by Allan Eckert, *Century of Conflict* by Joseph Lister Rutledge, and *The White and the Gold* by Thomas Costain. These books, full of scenery and adventure, bring history to life. And since these masters say it so well, I have quoted widely from their works in order to highlight the great feats of the partisans of New France. For even in these great works, the accomplishments of the partisans often become lost in the telling of the larger story of the colonial conflicts.

Modern-day American writers such as Andy Gallup, Doc Shaffer and I have tried to re-awaken and tell the story of the "underdog" New France. In following volumes, I hope to tell of Greysolon DuLhut and Nicholas Perrot of the early years, and Joseph de Léry, Paul and Joseph Marin, Legardeur de Saint-Pierre and Saint-Luc de La Corne, just to name a few. I sincerely hope that all history lovers and reenactors will enjoy reading about the "forgotten side," the side of the French.

To help the reader visualize the way of life and the living conditions of these tough men, I have included a brief section on trekking, which describes clothing, gear, food and techniques of eighteenth-century survival.

There is a statement in Charles Moore's *The Northwest Under Three Flags: 1635-1796*, in the beginning of Chapter One, which has influenced me to start writing this very book:

> *Often one catches glimpses of shadowy forms gliding among the whispering pines, or sees afar off a swift darting canoe skimming over clear waters, only to find that the name of that daring trader who has pushed into the unknown regions has disappeared as completely as the print of his snowshoe, or the swirl of his paddle.*

The partisan leaders have vanished forever, like the prints of their snowshoes and the swirls of their paddles.

The accounts of their lives must not.

Bob Bearor

❧ *TWO SPECIAL REENACTORS*

*A*ctually, all reenactors are very special people, spending thousands of dollars for their uniforms, outfits, muskets and equipment, driving hundreds of miles to events and dedicating their off-time hours to the research and promotion of history and the education of the public. Some of the most dedicated reenactors go above and beyond even this, devoting countless hours to planning and coordinating the events that are enjoyed so much by the participants and spectators.

Usually it is greatly appreciated. Fort Niagara, the premier French and Indian reenacting site since 1980, where eastern reenactors can link up with their counterparts from the western states, is the best example of a site that truly shows its "reenactor appreciation."

Fort Niagara has always treated its participants to coffee and doughnuts each morning, and a complete lunch on Saturday afternoons. Fortress Louisbourg generously and graciously supplied reenactors with all meals and also gave units pre-measured cartridges of black powder. Municipalities like the city of Plattsburgh, the Town of Ticonderoga, and the Village of Lake George, grateful for the publicity and business that we bring to them, show their appreciation by hosting reenactors' suppers. These small gestures are greatly appreciated, and we thank all of the sites that continue to support this wonderful and educational hobby of reenacting.

I am immensely proud to belong to the "brotherhood" of reenactors, and I would like to pay tribute to two very special reenactors to whom we on the French side owe a great deal: Jon Soule and Mike Malecki.

My personal reenacting experiences began in the 1970s, when I portrayed a *coureur de bois*. In the 1980s I took on the persona of a French partisan leader, and in the 1990s I joined *Les Compagnies Franches de la Marine* and served under Jon Soule at Fort Ticonderoga, Crown Point and Fort Number Four. I also served under Mike Malecki at Fort Niagara and Fortress Louisbourg. Since becoming an officer, I have also served with them in these later years, and I feel that they have personified the true French leadership of the 1700s. To the uninitiated, the role of commander is not what it may appear. It is NOT a lot of fun! It IS a lot of headaches! It is a position of responsibility, where a lot of things can go wrong, a lot of egos can get bruised, and a lot of blame, most of it undeserved, comes back to rest.

In the highly successful "Death of Lord Howe" event during the summer of 2001, while the French force lay in wait in a ravine for the arrival on the field of the British and Ranger troops, I glanced over my shoulder to hear muted voices and muffled laughter and saw Jon and Mike, sitting on their haunches, sharing a joke and a light moment with troops of their respective companies. They were having fun, enjoying the moment, and awaiting the battle. This time the "monkey" was off of their backs; I was the one in charge, and the awesome responsibility of the event was mine. I turned back, awaiting the arrival of the British troops, and I grinned also; today was my turn in the "barrel," they had been there before.

Jon Soule and Mike Malecki, along with Bruce Egli and Ray Washlaski, are some of the people who have really furthered the French side of the French and Indian War reenacting movement and made it come a long, long way. In many cases, it has been a hard, thank-you-less job.

Merci beaucoup, mes amis! Thanks from all of us!

❧ Acknowledgments

*T*he acknowledgment section of my books is very important to me. Through it I recognize and confirm those wonderful people who have helped make each book a success.

First and foremost, as always, should be family. My wife Holly, sons Cliff and Ted, and daughters Becky and Jenny, have always been there to help me through the sticking points, listening, prodding, and cajoling, they help keep me going to get it done.

Second only to family, my greatest "Thanks" goes to my good friend and editor, Roxanne Carlson. Roxanne's tremendous talent to turn a manuscript into a great book never ceases to amaze me. She is truly gifted and generous and makes writing a book a real pleasure.

A true friend, fellow author, historian, re-enactor, hunter and trekker, is George "Peskunck" Larrabee. George and I have shared many stories, sources, and campfires over the years, and together we have shared that knowledge with our readers, for their enjoyment and knowledge.

Peskunck, along with well-known Heritage artist, Joe Lee, and Ralph Mitchard from Great Britain, are responsible for the artwork in this book. Their skills help bring the stories to life for the reader. Thanks also to Mike Mason, who photographed the gorget for the book cover.

I am indebted to Steve Blanchard, former Director of the Ticonderoga Historical Society, for his kind words of praise.

The bulk of my research was done at the Ticonderoga Historical Society, and Steve not only was instrumental in helping me locate sources, but also deserves much credit for his tremendous patience, help, and hard work in the now famous "Death of Lord Howe" re-enactment in June of 2001 for the Town of Ticonderoga.

Likewise, "Thanks" goes to Mary Jane McFadden of Fort Necessity in western Pennsylvania, for her encouragement and help. Fort Necessity will be THE place to be in Spring of 2004, when the 250th anniversary of the French and Indian war commences there.

To Father Thomas of Fort Bon Secours, I am indebted for his help. After meeting at Fortress Louisbourg in 1999, Father Thomas presented me with a hardcover copy of Louise Phelps Kellogg's *The French Regime in Wisconsin and the Northwest* (now available in soft cover from Heritage Books, Inc.) This book was of tremendous help to me in fleshing out the life history of Charles-Michel Mouet de Langlade.

Deepest thanks and regrets go to Fred LaPann, my dear close friend, who shared so much with so many, and to whom the chapter on Sabbath Day Point is dedicated.

To my dear friend, Dick Weller, my hunting and shooting partner, and who, like Fred LaPann, shares his talents and knowledge freely with others. Thanks to the influence and help of Dick Weller, Roxanne and I were able to help Burt Loescher get his famous series of *The History of Rogers' Rangers* reprinted through Heritage Books, Inc. Already the first three volumes are available, with the much anticipated and long awaited *St. Francis Raid* due to come out shortly.

Last but not least, a special thanks to Heritage Books, Inc., and ALL of its wonderful employees. Working with Heritage is like working with family, and I am grateful to them for their help throughout the years.

Ted Bearor portrays Sieur Jacques LeMoyne de Ste. Hélène

1

SIEUR JACQUES LeMOYNE de STE. HÉLÈNE

❧ The Fabulous LeMoynes

*I*N ORDER TO TELL THE STORY OF STE. HÉLÈNE, A brief history of the famous LeMoyne family must also be included.

They have been dubbed by many great writers as the "fabulous LeMoynes," and rightfully so. No other family is there that I can compare in the history of Canada to this astonishing, marvelous and legendary brood.

There were eleven sons, ten of whom lived to maturity, and two daughters born to Charles LeMoyne. All ten of the sons would gain honor, prestige, and greatness in the history of New France.[1]

Charles LeMoyne was born in Dieppe, France, the son of an innkeeper.[2] He immigrated to New France when he was 17 years old and is first mentioned in the *Jesuit Relations* as an interpreter with the Hurons. He would become a fearless fighter against the Iroquois, who called him "Akouesson," and kept a torture stake reserved for his burning some day.[3] That day never came, as Charles LeMoyne ended up dying peacefully in his bed after a very eventful life.

Shortly after his arrival in New France, Charles LeMoyne was granted 50 arpents of land on the St. Lawrence River across from Montreal. An additional 90 arpents were later added upon his marriage to Catherine Primot in 1654.[4] As the years passed, Charles entered into the fur trade and prospered, using his profits to construct what eventually became one of the most important seigneuries of Canada. He and Catherine also were busy producing what became the fabulous family of LeMoynes.

The first son was named Charles, and he not only inherited his father's name, but also his keen instincts for business and financial dealings. He enlarged and developed his father's estate, now known as Longueuil, into a veritable fort and chateau with walls over 200 feet long, watch towers, a chapel, stables, and close by, a brewery. After the death of his father, Charles was called the Baron of Longueuil, and later became the Governor of the colony of New France for a brief time. He died in battle at Saratoga in 1729.[5]

In 1659 the second son, Jacques de Ste. Hélène was born. He will be the main subject of this chapter.

Third born, in 1661, was Pierre LeMoyne d'Iberville, who was destined to become the most famous of the fighting LeMoynes, both on land and sea.[6] His rise to fame began in 1686 when he accompanied the Chevalier Pierre de Troyes of Montreal in the expedition to seize the English forts at Hudson Bay. With Iberville were his brothers Ste. Hélène and Paul, also known as Maricourt.[7] The force left early in the spring of 1686, but instead of going up the usual route via the St. Lawrence from Quebec where they might be discovered, they chose to go up the Ottawa River, past Lake Abitibi and into the Abitibi River, coming into the southern portion of James Bay, where the objective, Fort Hayes, lay unaware. The English were sleeping soundly in the four-bastioned stockade, when Iberville and his brothers, with their men, climbed over the six-foot walls and silently gained control of the compound. When the gate was battered down with a ram, the garrison came rushing out, only to face the LeMoynes and their squad, waiting with aimed muskets. After taking Fort Hayes, the French force marched overland 40 leagues to Fort Rupert, capturing it with a similar attack at night by surprise. That same day, Iberville led a small party and captured the ship in the harbor whose cargo included Governor Bridgar of the Hudson Bay Company. The ten cannon from this vessel were used to lay siege to the next target, Fort Albany, which surrendered in July of that same year.[8]

In 1690, Iberville joined his brother Ste. Hélène at the attack on Schenectady. Later that same year, again with Ste. Hélène and brothers Longueuil and Maricourt, he took up arms at the siege and defense of Quebec under Governor Frontenac.[9]

In 1696, he commanded two ships and won a small battle off of the St. John River. Following that action he helped the Baron St. Castine in recapturing Pemaquid.[10]

Iberville's most famous battle expedition came in 1697, leading a squadron of ships into Hudson Bay. Fog and ice soon separated the ships, and Iberville found himself and crew alone on their 44-gun frigate, the *Pelican*. Arriving before the others of his squadron at the mouth of the Hayes River on September 5, Iberville spotted three sails bearing down upon him, and their intention did not appear friendly. They turned out to be the British ships, *Hampshire*, a 56-gun vessel, and two frigates, the *Daring* with 36 guns and the *Hudson Bay*, carrying 32 guns.[11]

Throwing retreat and caution to the wind, Iberville went straight to the attack. The first broadsides from the *Pelican* were well aimed and sent the big *Hampshire* straight to the bottom. Next in line came the *Hudson Bay*, which joined its sister ship and crew in an icy grave of water. The *Daring* did not live up to its name, and turning about she fled to safety, leaving Iberville and the crew of the badly damaged *Pelican* undisputed masters of Hudson Bay. Iberville and his force then proceeded to take the post of York Factory and renamed it Fort Bourban.[12] Because of his daring exploits and accomplishments, Iberville was awarded the Cross of St. Louis, the first Canadian-born soldier to receive the honor.[13]

From 1699 until his death in 1706, Iberville's adventures took him to what are now the southern United States and the Gulf of Mexico. In March of 1699 he found the mouth of the Mississippi River and followed it until reaching the place where he founded the settlement of New Orleans. Later he erected Fort Maurepas in Biloxi Bay, the first permanent post in Louisiana. He later founded and built Fort Louis de Mobile, on which the city of Mobile, Alabama, now stands. After seeing the settlements and forts take root, he proceeded to prowl the seas, sinking enemy ships and sacking the post and Isle of Nevis in the West Indies. He died of yellow fever aboard his flagship in Havana Harbor, a long way from the cold of northern Canada, and the warmth of the family home at Longueuil.[14]

Fourth in line was Paul LeMoyne de Maricourt, who gained his fame as the family ambassador and interpreter among the Indian tribes, who in return liked and accepted him, giving him the name "Taouistauisse," which meant "Little Bird always in motion."[15] Maricourt was with his brothers in the expeditions against Forts Albany and Rupert in Hudson Bay, and again with them at the siege of Quebec in 1690.[16] He was also a captain of French Marines and died in 1704 in an expedition against the Iroquois.

The fifth son was Francois LeMoyne de Bienville, born in 1666. Little is known of him except that he had the typical LeMoyne traits of courage and adventure, and was killed in action in 1691 while fighting against the Iroquois at Repentigny.[17]

The sixth of the sons was named Joseph LeMoyne de Serigny, born in 1668. He served in the French navy and was second in command of Iberville's fleet in the brilliant Hudson Bay conquest of 1697. Later in life, because of his maritime experience, he rose to become governor of a French naval base, where he is said to have served with much distinction.[18]

The seventh son was called Louis LeMoyne de Chateaugay. When he was only eighteen years old, he was killed in battle, charging an English fort (Nelson) in the Hudson Bay campaign with his brother Iberville.[19]

The eighth son was called Jean Baptiste LeMoyne de Bienville. He accompanied Iberville on his explorations to the Mississippi, and assumed command after Iberville's death. It was he who laid out the settlement of New Orleans and became and remained Governor of Louisiana for most of his life.[20]

The ninth son was Gabriel LeMoyne d'Assigny, born in 1681, who also took part in Iberville's Mississippi adventures, and who also died of yellow fever in San Domingo, in 1701.

The tenth and final son was Antoine LeMoyne de Chateaugay, born in 1683, and probably outlived all of the brothers, eventually becoming the Governor of French Guiana.[21]

Before ending this treatise of the fabulous LeMoynes, I would like to share some observations. Obviously, they were all skilled in the arts of war. They probably received such military and naval training, as did Iberville in the later 1670s and early 1680s.[22]

Another observation is the apparent grooming, or tutoring, of the sons by their father in leadership roles such as dealing with Indians. Each of them seemed to possess an innate, commanding presence among other men. This trait is evident in many great families of Canadians whose knowledge of warfare and diplomacy was passed down from father to son, and brother to brother. An example of this occurred in 1673 when Charles LeMoyne, the father, accompanied Count Frontenac to Cataraqui, where Fort Frontenac was built in front of the amazed Iroquois delegations. With Charles were his sons Longueuil, Ste. Hélène, and Iberville, who was at that time only twelve years old. Here in the shadows of the great Frontenac and their father, they learned first-hand how to deal with the Indians.

Finally, it seems that whenever more than one of the brothers were gathered, the action seemed to accelerate. It appears that sibling bond and rivalry spurned them on to be more daring. In all of the great fights and raids, more than one of the clan is present.

As author Thomas B. Costain mused in his excellent book, *The White and the Gold*, it is a pity that some servant or relative did not keep records of the childhood days of this rambunctious bunch of fire-eaters. As a father, I can relate to and wonder what it would have been like to hear their schemes and dreams, and to hear the complaints and praises of their neighbors and kin; to have heard the screams and protests of their two sisters when the inevitable teasing started, and the kind but firm voice of their mother, Catherine LeMoyne, as she asserted her matriarchal authority in the great home. It is indeed a shame that more information is not available to be known of this magnetic band of boys who grew to be Canada's great men.[23]

⚜ *Jacques LeMoyne de Ste. Hélène*

When Count Frontenac returned from France in 1689 for his second term as governor, he became painfully aware of the dire straits that the colony had fallen into since his departure seven years earlier. The succeeding governors' lack of foresight, coupled with timidity and bad judgment, had turned the colony into shambles, and the Iroquois had made those later governors into a mockery.

The uneasy peace that had reigned between the Iroquois and New France since Frontenac's departure was now completely broken. Iroquois were attacking, pillaging and killing everywhere. Worst of all was the calamity at the village of Lachine, not far from Montreal, where on a stormy August night in 1689, a force of nearly 1500 Iroquois warriors had put it to the torch, killing and torturing the helpless inhabitants. This grim massacre, the worst in the history of Canada, had stunned and numbed its people. New France was on the verge of collapse.[24]

Frontenac's return changed all of that. His powerful bearing inspired the *habitants* with confidence. A firm believer in action, and that the best defense is a good offense, he decided to strike back immediately to stun the enemy and boost the morale of the Canadians.

He had to pick carefully both the targets and the men to lead the raids. The targets were easy. A strike was planned against the Province of New York at Albany, against the Province of Massachusetts at Casco Bay in what is now the State of Maine, and against the settlement of Salmon Falls on the Maine-New Hampshire border.

A Soldier of Ste. Hélène's Force.
(Illustration by Ralph Mitchard.)

Now, he had to choose men who could lead these punitive strikes. They had to be men of physical and mental toughness; men who would not let the harshness of northern winters, length of travel, lack of supplies, or the capriciousness of their Indian allies stop them from attaining their objectives. Frontenac's choices to lead the men of New France proved his ability as governor.

The force leaving from Three Rivers, bound for the border settlement of Salmon Falls, would be led by Francois Hertel de LaFresniere, whose reputation for daring and courage earned him the nickname, "The Hero" among his fellow Canadians. His sons would also be there, along with his nephews.[25]

The force leaving Quebec would be under the command of Rene Robineau de Portneuf, a veteran of raids and ambushes in Acadia. Before his arrival at Casco Bay, his force would be augmented by some 36 men led by Hertel who would be coming from Salmon Falls, and Baron St. Castine with his hand-picked force of Abenaki warriors.[26]

The third force would leave from Montreal and would be led by more of Canada's great. Nicholas d'Ailleboust de Mantet had been with Greysolon DuLhut when they succeeded in destroying a large party of Iroquois warriors on the Lake of the Two Mountains, shortly after the massacre at Lachine. Also leading the expedition would be Jacques LeMoyne de Ste. Hélène, second son of the fabulous clan. Accompanying them were the LeMoyne brothers, Iberville and Bienville.[27]

It is here we are given a description of Ste. Hélène by the famous author Joseph Lister Rutledge.

Ste. Hélène was the most attractive of the ten LeMoyne brothers. He had less of arrogance and more of friendliness. He was a shrewd and determined fighter, but he added a gift of laughter that softened the harshness of action. He and Iberville were inseparable until Ste. Hélène's untimely death at the age of thirty-one made separation final. They had been together in most of their adventures, first one and then the other in superior command. It had not yet appeared that of all that close-knit family, Iberville was to become the greatest, as Ste. Hélène might have been the best liked. Ste. Hélène was a devoted family man, a good husband and father. Six years before he had married Jeanne Carion, and had three children by her.

For all of his outward gentleness and humor, for all the kindliness so noticeable that even the Indians spoke with gratitude of how he had refused to take advantage during the heat of an attack and had let thirty possible prisoners escape. He had a reputation for gallantry, enterprise and determination. For this expedition, he would need all three.[28]

❧ *Schenectady 1690*

Although Frontenac's planned attacks were to be simultaneous, it didn't quite work out that way. The Montreal force was ready before the others and had departed earlier. It was composed of 160 French and 140 Indians. The French of the party were typical *coureurs de bois*, of whom Parkman says, "As the sea is the sailor's element, so the forest was theirs. Their merits were hardihood and skill in woodcraft."[29] They would need lots of both traits to pull off this raid.

In the depth of a brutal Canadian winter the force started out from Montreal, heading down the frozen St. Lawrence River, crossing through the forest to Chambly, then up the Richelieu to the icy vastness of Lake Champlain. Here, at the insistence of the Indians, they stopped to hold a council. The destination, at the suggestion of Frontenac, had been kept secret until now, known only to the leaders. When learning of the plan to attack Albany, the Indians grew scornful and asked derisively, "How long is it that the French have grown so bold?"[30] Here was a time and a place where the mission could have fallen apart like so many others had before. But Frontenac knew his leaders and had picked them well. Ste. Hélène stepped to the front, assuaged the Indians of their doubts and fears, and told them that the French were men, and to prove it they would take Albany or die in the attempt. His words and demeanor, along with the tough, lean looks of the Canadians, must have served to convince the Indians. This was not an idle boast. The force moved onward.

What compelled these men to make this expedition? Was it love of God, King and Country? Was it hatred for the English and a burning desire for revenge? Was it a chance for adventure and an opportunity to relieve the boredom of everyday life? Was it the desire to pillage and come away with riches and booty, perhaps? Probably it was a combination of all. But whatever the reasons, their fervor must have grown quite cooler on the long, cold march towards Albany. Sometime in the following weeks, they all must have questioned it in their minds, and perhaps it was brought up at a campfire at night. It would be at times like this, that Ste. Hélène was at his best, encouraging, exhorting, and pleading with his Canadian countrymen, but even more so with the Indian allies of New France.

About halfway through the march, the gods of ill fortune made their appearance. As if the journey were not bad and tiring enough, as the weary men drove themselves onward through the bitter cold and snow, a January thaw set upon them with all its added nightmares. They were forced to

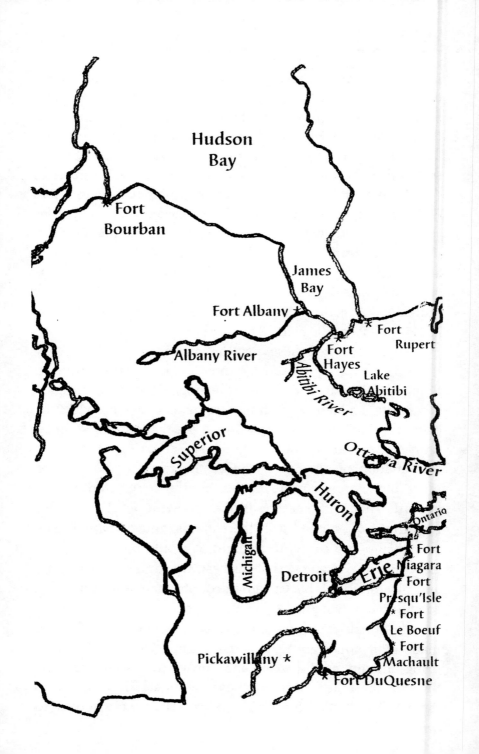

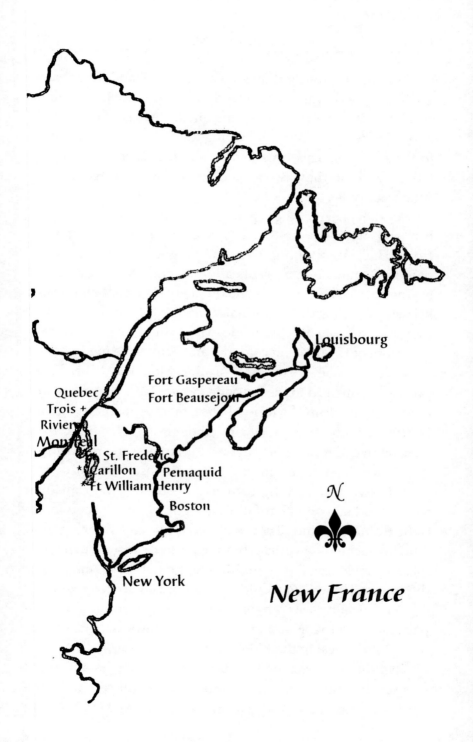

wade knee-deep through melted snow, mud, and icy streams. Their progress was painful and slow, and each day more precious rations were being consumed.[31] At last they came to a fork in the trail; one path leading towards Albany, the other to Schenectady. This time there was no council. Albany was too strong for these weakened men. They started toward Schenectady.[32]

As they neared their goal, the weather changed again, bringing with it a cold, gusty snowstorm. The men were frozen, half-dead with hunger and fatigue. A Canadian scout named Gigniers had gone ahead to reconnoiter and returned saying that he had seen no one on guard, and that all persons seemed to be inside.[33] Originally planning to attack the next morning, a decision was made. They simply could not take any more of the freezing cold; the attack must be made now.[34]

Crossing the frozen ice of the Mohawk River, they proceeded onward to the palisaded town. Here they were met by two sentinels in the form of snowmen! Apparently no one in Schenectady had given any thought to an attack from Canada in the middle of winter.[35] Surely no sane man would come over 200 miles in these conditions. Normally they would have had nothing to worry about, but the Canadian force who had come that far, that night, were not men in the right frame of mind. They were starving and freezing, and whether Schenectady had been guarded by snowmen or a force of men on the walls, it would not have made any difference. These men would not be stopped on this night.

Schenectady was an oblong village, surrounded by a palisade with two gates: one facing east towards Albany, the other facing west to the Mohawk country.[36]

Iberville was assigned to find the Albany gate and bar it to prevent any escape, but somehow he missed it in the darkness that night. Ste. Hélène and Mantet led the force

Schenectady Stockade. (Illustration by Joe Lee.)

quietly inside and separated, one group going to the left, the other to the right. They led their men in two files around the village houses and between the stockaded walls. When the two groups met at the far end, the village was completely surrounded.[37] The signal was given and the attack began; doors were burst open, fusils fired, and tomahawks flashed. There was little resistance, so complete was the surprise — except at the blockhouse where a Lt. Talmadge and his militia were stationed. They tried to make a fight of it, but the doors were forced and the defenders were killed or taken prisoner.[38] At another strong house of resistance, a Canadian named Montigni was stopped and twice wounded trying to force his way inside, but Ste Hélène and his men came up quickly, forced the door, and put to death all of the combatants in the house.[39] After two hours of fire and carnage, it was all over. The French had completely destroyed the village and its defenders, and now basked in the warmth of the houses, gorging themselves with all the food they could find. Prisoners were rounded up, many women and children set free, and all the booty, food, and provisions that could be found were loaded upon the forty horses found in the village, and the force prepared to return to Canada. Knowing that at least one man had escaped (Simon Schermerhorn), and would give warning to the village of Albany, the entire settlement of Schenectady was set ablaze, and the long, hard march to Canada began.[40]

The Siege And Battle Of Quebec

October 1690

The next battle in which Ste. Hélène participated would be his most famous and, unfortunately, his last. It was at the siege and battle of Quebec in 1690, commanded by Governor Frontenac, against the New England forces led by Sir William Phips.

Phips is one of the most colorful and interesting figures of history. Born in a family of 26 children, he was tough, enterprising, and a natural leader. Early in his youth he apprenticed as a ship's carpenter and learned this and other maritime crafts well. Marrying a wealthy widow by the name of Mary Hull, he found himself in a position to advance his personal standing and to satisfy his thirst for fortune, fame, and power.

Fortune came first. Having heard rumors and tales of incredible wealth lying in sunken Spanish ships, Phips came up with a daring plan to salvage such treasures. Sailing to England, he gained a hearing and induced the Admiralty to adopt his scheme.[41] A frigate was given to him and he sailed to the West Indies, where a fruitless search and a leaky frigate caused him to abandon the quest and return empty-handed.

However, the information he gained on that trip produced another meeting and this time he found himself backed by the Duke of Albemarle and other nobility. This expedition proved successful and he found the shipwreck and raised over three hundred thousand pounds of gold, silver, and jewels.[42] He recompensed his benefactors, his crew, the Royal coffers, and himself. For this feat he was given a knighthood.

Because of the three winter raids sent by Frontenac, the English colonists became furious and somewhat united in their desire for revenge. Cotton Mather, the zealous, witch-hunting preacher of Puritan Boston and close friend of Phips, argued, "Of all who agreed sensibly, Canada must be reduced." Phips needed no further prodding.[43]

In April Phips sailed from Nantasket to attack the French fort at Port Royal in Acadia, with eight ships and over 700 men. Coming into the harbor, he trained the ships' guns upon the fort and demanded its immediate surrender. The timid commander, Governor Meneval, had neither enough men nor courage to stand up to Phips, and meekly and quickly surrendered. Meneval's greatest concerns were not of the fort and the harbor, but of the supplies and goods, particularly his own. These items included such finery as "silver forks and spoons, two dozen shirts, three new wigs, four nightcaps with lace edging, and six vests of dimity," among other things. While the terms were being agreed to, some of Phips' men found out that some merchants had carried off their personal property to be hidden in the forest. Phips thought this a sufficient pretext for plundering the merchants, imprisoning the troops, and desecrating the church. "We cut down the cross," writes one of his followers, "rifled their church, pulled down their altar, and broke their images." The houses of the two priests were also pillaged. Because of these violations, Phips was forever branded as a pirate by the French. The English king rewarded Phips for this venture by making him Governor of Massachusetts, two years later.[44]

As the colonies looked to further reduce Canada, a two-pronged plan of attack was developed. The first prong, a land attack, would proceed from Albany up through the Champlain valley, and would attack Montreal. It would be commanded by Fitz-John Winthrop of Connecticut and

Robert Livingston of New York.[45] The second prong of the invasion would come against Quebec from New England, in the form of a force sailing from Boston and commanded by none other than Sir William Phips, who agreed that "The plan is well formed and I am the best man in Boston to handle it."[46]

As expected, the Reverend Cotton Mather had the populace thinking of this endeavor as a great crusade. "A proclamation was issued, calling the people to repentance; a day of fasting was ordained; and as Mather expressed it, 'the wheel of prayer was kept in continual motion.'"[47]

The stage was now set for one of the greatest battles in Canada's history. Phips' great fleet sailed from Boston in August of 1690 with thirty-two ships and over twenty-two hundred men. Phips' confidence was contagious.

> No thought of failure crossed his mind and, just as he believed in himself, the men who followed him believed too. Without rhyme or reason, there seems to have developed among the English an overwhelming assurance of victory. It was supported by no evidence unless one saw a parallel between Port Royal and Quebec, between the seventy men captained by Meneval of the six vests of dimity and the four nightcaps with lace edging, and Frontenac, the tough old eagle at Quebec, with the LeMoynes and the DuLhuts, and the Perrots at his back.[48]

At this point, things began to go sour for the English land force under Winthrop. Following Wood Creek to its joining with the waters of Lake Champlain, disputes among the commanders arose. Supplies that had been promised, were slim and none. There were no canoes available and smallpox was breaking out. The commanders finally agreed to turn around and head back home. So ended the first effort of the three-pronged threat. Only a small force, led by Captain John

Schuyler, advanced into Canada, and raided the small village of La Prairie.[49]

During the winter, Frontenac had employed gangs of men in cutting timber in the forests, hewing it into palisades, and dragging it to Quebec. Nature had fortified the upper town on two sides by cliffs almost inaccessible, but it was open to attack in the rear; and Frontenac gave his first thoughts to strengthening this, its only weak side. The work began as soon as the frost was out of the ground, and before midsummer it was well advanced. Towards the end of July, Frontenac left the Town Major, Prevost, to finish the fortifications, and with the Intendant Champigny, went up to Montreal.[50]

While Frontenac was at Montreal, Phips' fleet was making its way to Quebec. Shortly after Schuyler's attack and retreat from La Prairie, Frontenac received a message at 3 o'clock on October 10 from Prevost, that Quebec was about to be attacked. Frontenac left immediately in a small vessel that leaked horribly. Switching to a canoe, he was frantically paddled downstream with all haste. The next day he was met by another canoe dispatched from Quebec with news that the English fleet had been seen near Tadoussac. Sending word back to Montreal, he ordered its governor, Calliéres, to follow immediately, mustering all forces along the way. In my mind, the true, unsung heroes of Canada in those dramatic days were the unnamed *voyageurs* who sped Frontenac to Quebec in the nick of time, and Major Prevost, who had driven all available men in Quebec to complete the fortifications in time. "He had indeed accomplished wonders."[51]

Frontenac had arrived on the morning of the fourteenth and the city, which was showing signs of panic, composed itself under the united efforts of Frontenac and the aged and crippled Bishop Laval, who came out of retirement to be with his flock when it needed him most.

Early in the morning of October 16, the fog lifted off the cold St. Lawrence River, and there in the basin of Quebec, was Phips and his fleet. As the sun rose, it shimmered upon the rock of Quebec in all its glory, and the hills beyond were bathed in the bright, vibrant colors of autumn.

Frontenac was like a chess player, always looking one or two moves ahead of his opponent. Knowing the English penchant for protocol, he correctly anticipated that they would send an envoy with surrender terms before any actual attack. Intending to confuse and deceive the delegation, Frontenac brought his leaders together and ordered them to be dressed in their finest. When the longboat carrying the messenger of Phips pulled away from the flagship, canoes were dispatched to meet it halfway. They escorted it to the quay, where Major Prevost was waiting. Blindfolding the subaltern, Prevost purposely led him in a roundabout way, over and through obstacles and barricades and groups of soldiers were marched back and forth across his path, as he climbed to the upper town.[52]

The young officer was so completely fooled by this stratagem that he later told his leader, "It is a mighty town where I have been, Sir, the garrison is so strong that a step cannot be taken without rubbing shoulders with some rude person. In the great room where I handed your letter to His Excellency, the men were dressed so splendidly that it made small difference taking the cloth from my eyes, I was so dazzled by looking at them."[53]

In that dark paneled room with open windows and gold chandeliers stood the great men of Canada; the men who had made it and who would now defend it. They were dressed in their finest, with gold and silver lace, perukes, powders, plumes and ribbons. Fine swords were held about their waists by silken sashes. There were no smiles on the lean, hard, weathered faces of these men—only the promise in their eyes of a bloody battle without any quarter.

They were grouped about their leader, Frontenac, who had on either side of him the Bishop and the Intendant, and the group at their backs was impressive: De Ramesay, Subercase, Valrenne, Vaudreuil, Mantet, Hertel, and the two oldest LeMoyne brothers, Longueuil and Ste. Hélène. Slipping up the north channel, back from Hudson Bay, came the younger brothers, Iberville and Maricourt, in time for the fight. That evening Callieres would arrive and bring with him DuLhut, Durantaye, Perrot, and 800 men.[54]

Frontenac listened to the surrender demands patiently. When Phips' envoy had finished, he demanded Frontenac's reply within an hour, and showed him his watch, or face "the peril that would ensue." A cry of indignation arose and Valrenne called out loudly that Phips was nothing but a pirate, and his man ought to be hanged.[55]

Frontenac did not keep the envoy waiting another moment, and at the end of his reply told the subaltern, "I will answer your General only by the mouths of my cannon, that he may learn that a man like me is not to be summoned after this fashion. Let him do his best, I will do mine."[56] The blindfold was replaced, and the young messenger was sent back to Sir William Phips.

The gauntlet had now been thrown. Quebec was not to suffer the same fate as Port Royal.

After sending the ultimatum to Frontenac, and receiving his terse reply, Phips was astounded. He had really believed that Quebec would not have opposed him. As the day passed, his opportunity for assault did also, as the tide was against him. For the rest of that day and the next, Phips and his second-in-command, Major Walley, planned the siege. It was to be a two-part attack with the great ships of Sir William Phips' fleet to sail in and cannonade the front of the town, while Major Walley would lead a force that would land on the Beauport shore, cross the St. Charles River, and attack Quebec from the rear.

On Tuesday, which was extremely gusty and blustering, Phips and Walley still lay at anchor finalizing the siege plans. One of the smaller vessels, sent in to examine a landing place at Beauport, ended up being grounded in the mud flats. The Canadians promptly plied her with bullets and brought a cannon to bear on her, and would have destroyed her had she not been able to get away when the tide rose again.[57]

At 11 a.m. on Wednesday, the French heard the drums and fifes of Phips' fleet, and the repeated shouts of "God save King William!" roaring from the throats of the New Englanders. Watching through their telescopes, the French in Quebec saw the English troops leave in the longboats and make for the Beauport shore, over 1300 in number, and commanded by Major Walley.[58]

Meanwhile, Sir William Phips left his moorings and took his largest ships to bombard the town. Phips' gunners fired with everything they had, and were answered in kind from the guns of Quebec. So rapid and fierce was the firing that Baron LaHonton compared it to volleys of musketry; and old officers, veterans of many sieges in Europe, declared that they had never seen the like.[59]

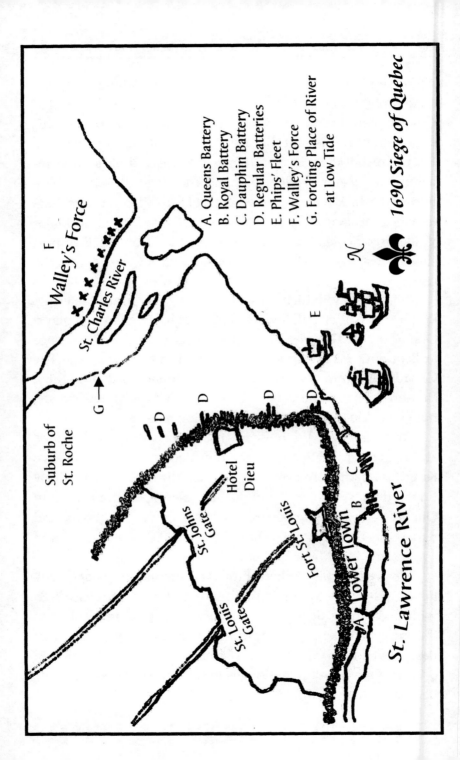

1690 Siege of Quebec

A. Queens Battery
B. Royal Battery
C. Dauphin Battery
D. Regular Batteries
E. Phips' Fleet
F. Walley's Force
G. Fording Place of River
   at Low Tide

As the tremendous roar of these explosions reverberated from the heights and mountains, the land force under Walley began wading ashore through the slimy mud and water. They formed up in companies and proceeded inland. On observing this, Frontenac dispatched over 300 sharpshooters under Ste. Hélène to meet and hold them in check. A battalion of troops followed; but long before they could reach the spot, Ste. Hélène's men, with militia from the neighboring parishes and a band of Huron warriors from Lorette, threw themselves into the thickets along the front of the enemy, and opened a distant but galling fire upon the compact bodies of the New Englanders.[60] After a see-saw battle which lasted most of the day, Walley withdrew his men back to the St. Charles River to await much-needed supplies from the vessels.

Phips lay quiet until daybreak, when Frontenac sent a shot to awaken him, and the cannonade began again. Ste. Hélène had returned from Beauport, and along with brother Maricourt, took charge of the two batteries of the Lower Town, aiming the guns with excellent precision against the four largest ships of the fleet. One of the shots cut the flagstaff of the Admiral, and the flag with the cross of St. George fell into the river. It drifted with the tide towards the shore, whereupon several Canadians paddled out in a birch canoe, secured it, and brought it back in triumph.[61]

The night of Thursday found Phips' fleet badly damaged by the fire of Ste. Hélène and his French gun crews, and so he was forced to withdraw out of range and repair the damage. Walley's force had not advanced and the men were suffering greatly, as that night was so cold that an inch of ice formed on the St. Charles River. The ships that had been sent to Walley's aid unloaded six field guns—twelve-pounders that weighed about eight hundred pounds each and promptly got mired in the oozing mud. About the only things that helped Walley and his men were the barrels of gunpowder and food that amounted to little more than a biscuit per man.[62]

Disgusted and discouraged, Walley went to see his commander the next morning. While they were in conference, Walley's force decided to move on its own and try again to take Quebec. As the force advanced, the Canadians came down to meet them. What started as a small series of skirmishes, developed rather quickly into the makings of a sizeable battle. Frontenac dispatched three battalions of regular troops to support the Canadians, while Ste. Hélène and Longueuil opened fire on them from the neighboring thickets. Walley's advance parties were driven back at this hot encounter, with the chief loss falling again on the compacted groups of New Englanders.[63] It was at this scene that Longueuil was stunned by a spent bullet, but Ste. Hélène received a wound in the leg which would prove mortal.

It is interesting to read about the wounding and subsequent death of Ste. Hélène from the great writers of history. Joseph Lister Rutledge states:

> Ste. Hélène, the second of the LeMoyne brothers, was in charge of the attack, and with him was his older brother Longueuil. LeMoyne-like, they were in the thick of it, and for once their fabulous luck had run out. Longueuil was hit and down, fortunately it was a spent bullet which stunned, but did little permanent damage. When they came to Ste. Hélène, it was different. There was a great hole in his thigh and these men were familiar enough with wounds to recognize its seriousness. They were able to get him away and back to a bed in the Hotel-Dieu. There was a week or two of misery ahead of him, and then rest in a quiet spot in the garden of that house of God.[64]

This would suggest that either the wound turned gangrenous, or Ste. Hélène died of some infection.

Thomas Costain relates:

In the meantime the land forces had not yet crossed the St. Charles River and were now making an effort to get over the ford. Ste. Hélène, who had moved from one point of need to another, had taken charge of the fighting along the river, and was mortally wounded at the same moment that his elder brother Charles was hit by a spent bullet. The death of the gallant Ste. Hélène was the worst loss the French cause sustained, for the English effort was suspended the next day, and the weary troops taken back to the ships.[65]

Finally, Charlevoix says in his description:

In this second action we had two men killed and four wounded, including, among the latter, the two commandants, who were always fighting with their usual valor at the head of their men; M. de Longueuil got off with a pretty severe contusion; but Ste. Hélène, his brother, wishing to take a prisoner, received a musket ball in the knee. The wound did not appear dangerous, but he died nevertheless, a few days after, to the great regret of his colony, who lost in him one of the most amiable cavaliers and bravest men it ever possessed.[66]

A few days later, the siege of Quebec was lifted and Sir William Phips and his grand fleet slunk back to Boston, to endure what old Governor Bradstreet would describe as "The awful frown of God."

Quebec was torn between mourning for Ste. Hélène and the other brave men who had died in her defense, and rejoicing for her deliverance from the Puritan heretics who had promised to sack the town, and had promised to kill the Jesuit priests and "cut off their ears to make necklaces."[67]

The captured flag of Phips' ship was borne to the cathedral in triumph; the Bishop sang the Te Deum; and amid the firing of cannon, the image of the Virgin was carried to each church and chapel in the city by a procession, in which priests, people, and troops all took part. The day closed with a grand bonfire in honor of Frontenac.[68]

So ends the story of Jacques LeMoyne de Ste. Hélène, fearless partisan fighter and leader of New France, hero of the great siege and battle of Quebec in 1690, and first of the fabulous LeMoynes to die in battle. Without a doubt, he was one of Canada's greatest. ⚜

Notes to Chapter One

[1] Costain, p. 379
[2] Costain, p. 208
[3] Parkman, p. 106
[4] Costain, p. 209
[5] Ibid
[6] Parkman, p. 388
[7] Parkman, p. 132
[8] Parkman, p. 133
[9] Parkman, p. 210
[10] Parkman, p. 380
[11] Parkman, p. 391
[12] Parkman, p. 391
[13] Chartrand, p. 94
[14] Rutledge, pp. 156-157
[15] Costain, p. 381
[16] Rutledge, pp 111, 156
[17] Parkman, p. 288
[18] Costain, p. 381. (*Note: de Serigny's 1687 death date in Costain is apparently a typographical error*)
[19] Rutledge, p. 156
[20] Parkman, p. 394
[21] Costain, pp 379-382
[22] Chartrand, p. 93
[23] Costain, p. 382
[24] Parkman, pp 178-179
[25] Charlevoix, p. 133
[26] Charlevoix, p. 130
[27] Charlevoix, pp 121-122
[28] Rutledge, p. 84
[29] Parkman, p. 209
[30] Parkman, p. 210
[31] Parkman, p. 211
[32] Parkman, p. 211, Charlevoix, p. 123

33 Parkman, p. 212
34 Charlevoix, p. 124
35 Parkman, p. 213
36 Parkman, p. 212
37 Charlevoix, p. 124
38 Parkman, p. 214
39 Charlevoix, p. 125
40 Parkman, p. 217
41 Parkman, p. 241
42 Parkman, p. 242
43 Rutledge, p. 106
44 Parkman, pp 237-243
45 Rutledge, p. 106
46 Rutledge, p. 103
47 Parkman, p. 245
48 Rutledge, p. 109
49 Parkman, p. 257
50 Parkman, p. 252
51 Parkman, p. 259
52 Parkman, pp 264-265
53 Rutledge, p. 112
54 Parkman, p. 265; Costain, p. 442; Rutledge, pp 110-111
55 Parkman, p. 267
56 Parkman, p. 268
57 Parkman, p. 270
58 Parkman, p. 271
59 Parkman, p. 273
60 Parkman, p. 271
61 Parkman, pp 273-274
62 Rutledge, p. 114
63 Parkman, p. 276
64 Rutledge, p. 116
65 Costain, pp. 445-446
66 Charlevoix, p. 180
67 Parkman, p. 281
68 Parkman, p. 283

2

LEARNING FROM TREKKING

❖ *Recreating A Winter Journey Today*

*T*HE CANADIANS AND THE INDIANS WOULD HAVE outfitted themselves similarly. Each man would have carried his own fusil, powder flask, knives and tomahawk. Clothing would have been worn in layers of wool and skins. Capotes, watch coats, or blankets were used in severe weather and for sleeping in at night. For traveling they would have been lightly dressed in wool shirts, leggings, and breechclouts to avoid overheating and sweating, the real killers and causes of exposure, or hypothermia. Mittens were indispensable, as were wool stockings, scarves, and wool hats, or *tuques*. Moccasins would have been well greased and perhaps lined with wool, fur, or the hollow hair of a deer. Each man had his snowshoes, or *raquettes* as they were called, and perhaps each had some form of ice creepers or *grappins* for traveling on the ice of frozen lakes and rivers. We are told that they pulled sleds (different than sledges) or toboggans behind them, which would have been loaded with extra blankets and provisions. How many men in a group pulled a sled is something we are not sure of even today.

The Canadians called the sleds or toboggans, *traines*.

The traine is a thin plank, six to nine feet in length, and twelve to fifteen inches in width. It is bent at one end in a half circle, called a hood, to which a strap called a collar is attached—made of birch withes about eighteen feet long. The center part is about three or four inches wide and sixteen to eighteen inches long. This collar is used to haul a load. The thick middle piece of the collar rests on the forehead, or sometimes slantingly across the chest and shoulders. The traine has, down its length and sides, sinews of animal hide into which a cord is laced to hold the goods loaded on the traine. Two or three hundred leagues can be covered in this way over the snow and ice.[1]

In my own experiences of trekking, I prefer using the tumpline across the forehead to carry a load, whether it be a pack or a traine. I do not like the constriction caused by straps across my chest and shoulders; also, the forehead tumpline is a lot quicker to disengage from, if an emergency occurs. Dragging a traine or toboggan full of provisions on a frozen lake or river is one thing, dragging it behind you through the forest is quite another. It is, to put it mildly, a real nightmare, and coming down a grade or slope, it has a mind of its own. Most of the time it wants to run you over, get tangled up, or run away on its own. The only way to prevent this is to have someone else hold it with another rope at the back. For short winter trips (up to three days), my trekking companions and I opt to carry our gear in packs. We firmly believe that the forces of French and Indians who made these journeys in the depth of winter did so in the following way:

Probably every fourth or fifth man would have pulled a traine which would have been loaded with extra food,

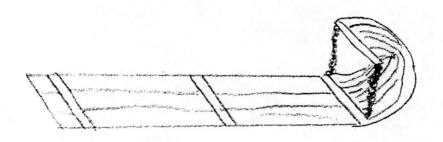

Toboggan or *Traine*

Used by Amerindians from pre-historic times. Used and
adapted by the French in Canada.

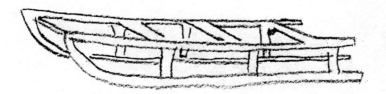

Sled or Sledge

Commonly used in the 18th century.
The runners kept the upper part and its cargo above the water
that sometimes lay on the ice surface after a mid-winter thaw.
(Like those used on Rigaud de Vaudreuil's winter 1757
expedition against Fort William Henry.)

On the march to Schedectady.

Cliff and Holly Bearor demonstrate
18th-century winter camping.

clothing, blankets and tarps to protect the provisions from the elements and for sleeping under at night in extremely inclement weather. These squads, or groups of men, would have taken turns at breaking trail and pulling the sled for one another. Some of their equipment would have been carried in individual packs or knapsacks as we do today. But every man would not have been carrying a full size axe or camp kettle for cooking food. Those were the types of gear that would have been placed on the sled to lighten and displace the overall weight for the group.

Traveling on snowshoes in winter for any length of distance and time is a very physically demanding venture. When attempting to march through three or four feet of soft snow, it becomes necessary for a group of men to "break trail" for one another. Simply told, breaking trail is done this way:

In a large party of men like the force led by Ste. Helene, three, four, or five men would walk abreast of each other as much as conditions and terrain permitted, packing the snow down for a hundred yards or so, until they became fatigued. They would then step off to the side, letting the rest go past, taking their place at the rear of the column. As the line of men progresses along, the trail becomes more solidly packed and much easier to walk on. By the time the twentieth man in line comes along, the going is much easier. By the time the end of the column approaches, it is a veritable piece of cake. By alternating thusly, the march can be continued for hours without undue fatigue.

The men would begin their march early in the day, to make as much time and distance in the daylight hours as possible. They would eat cold foodstuffs along the march, probably biscuits and breads made the night before. Biscuits were a special kind of bread that is baked until dry. They were often round and flattened and hard, and usually had to be rehydrated with soup to be enjoyed. Dried peas, as well as pemmican, kept very well and were the traditional bases for soup. They would travel most of the day with very few stops until an hour before dark, when they would make their camp, or bivouac. While some men would take the axes and begin to cut down firewood, others would be fanning out to cut down evergreen boughs to make beds with, while still others would be clearing away the snow and ice down to the bare ground, to make places for the huge fires to be built. Ideally they would try to use a large boulder or downed tree trunk for a reflector, lacking these they would simply build one out of stacked logs. It was important to dig down to the frozen earth when building the fire pit, so that the melting snow from the heat of the fire would not extinguish the much-needed blaze.

When we do our eighteenth-century recreation of these trips, we are usually out from three to ten days. Our gear and foods are exactly what they would have used over two hundred years ago.

But there are differences—*big* differences—between our trips of today and those of two hundred years ago. And we are quite aware of that fact. While our trips today usually last less than a week, the march from Montreal to Schenectady took 23 days. One way.[2] While we are able to pack and carry enough food for a week, it is much different than carrying enough food for a month. While we are able to hole up in real bad weather and wait it out, they could not. Every day the supplies were dwindling and they just couldn't pack it up and go home. They had an objective to achieve and to accomplish it they had to push on, each day, every day, regardless of weather. They could not take any more time than was absolutely necessary for fear of being discovered and warning being carried ahead. Also, there is the factor of mental stress to be considered. While we are doing this for the fun and knowledge, they were in real danger of losing their lives at any moment, whether from fatigue, starvation, or accident. And they knew at the end of the journey they would engage in a real life-and-death battle that could go either way. Lastly, after the attack, they would have to make the same long, backbreaking journey back to Canada, and safety.

Snowshoes – various *raquettes* used by French Indians.
Courtesy Adirondack Visitors Interpretive Center,
Newcomb, New York, and the Adirondack Museum
in Blue Mountain Lake, New York.

❖ *Notes to Chapter Two*

[1] Gallup and Shaffer, pp. 69-70
[2] Charlevoix, p. 124

Cliff Bearor portrays Sieur Charles-Michel de Langlade

3

SIEUR CHARLES-MICHEL de LANGLADE

C HARLES-MICHEL DE LANGLADE'S LINEAGE AND life seem to embody and give real meaning to the phrase "French and Indian War."

Langlade, in my opinion, epitomizes New France, the blending of the old with the new, a true son of the soil, or the forest, if you will.

Langlade's military heritage starts with his grandfather who was an officer in the regiment Carignon-Salieres, which came to Canada in 1665 to quell the Iroquois problems. Langlade's father, Augustin, was an officer in Les Compagnies Franches de La Marine.[1] Langlade's mother was an Ottawa woman known in her youth as La Blanche, probably because of the lightness of her skin. She was baptized as Domitelle, and in 1728, already a widow from a previous marriage, married Augustin de Langlade. The next year, 1729, their only child Charles-Michel was born. Domitelle was the sister of an Ottawa chief named Nissowaquet, also called La Fourche.[2] Langlade, with the military background of his father, was further educated by the Jesuits at Mackinac.[3] Added to this was the Indian culture of his mother's family and friends, and the person that evolved embodied the best and most fearsome traits of both cultures.

Charles' adventures started very early in his youth and it became apparent to many, that here was a boy destined for greatness.

> At the age of ten, Langlade gained a military reputation when he was summoned by his uncle, Chief La Fourche, to take part in a war party against the Chickasaws. La Fourche had dreamt that the enemy could only be put to rout by having Langlade accompany him on the expedition. A dream, in the Ottawa culture, was a powerful sign not to be disobeyed. If his father was apprehensive about having his young son travel to Tennessee with a war party, he had little choice about the matter, Augustin reportedly questioned his son about the Ottawas' request and then said, "You must go with your Uncle; but never let me hear of your showing any marks of cowardice."[4]

Charles Moore, in *The Northwest Under Three Flags: 1635-1796*, tells the same story with a few different details:

> In May 1729, Charles-Michel de Langlade was born and duly baptized. From the energetic and faithful missionary priest, Father DuJaunay, young Langlade obtained the beginnings of an education in letters; and at an age before boys usually leave the nursery he took his first lessons in Indian warfare. In 1734, when the French were seeking the aid of the Upper Lake savages in their war against the English traders north of the Ohio, The Fork (La Fourche) moved by a superstition not unknown even in these days, refused to take up the hatchet unless he were allowed to carry with him his five years old

grandson, in the capacity of what now would be known as a mascot; and the father, on being entreated, sent his son upon the war-path with the injunction never to dishonor a brave name. Never was paternal blessing better deserved or more carefully heeded; and the scalps brought back to adorn the wigwams of Michilimackinac testified abundantly to the success of the expedition. The superstitious Indians came to look upon young Langlade as one on whom a great manitou smiled; and from that day his influence over the savages exceeded that of any of his fellows.[5]

From that day forward, the name, Charles-Michel de Langlade, would become legend.

❧ *Pickawillany 1752*

Pickawillany, site of present-day Piqua, Ohio, was becoming a thorn in the side of New France. Since the Céloron Expedition in 1749, which was ordered to re-affirm French interests, alliances, and land claims throughout the Ohio valley and adjacent lands, the French not only met with rebuff, but undisguised hostility when dealing with the Indians who gathered at Pickawillany. The biggest problem was in fact the leader of these gathered tribes of Indians, predominantly Miami, a chief known collectively as Unemakemi, Memeskia, La Demoiselle, or mostly, "Old Briton," a name which he seemed to relish.[6]

As the years passed, "Old Briton's" tolerance of the French grew less and his embracing of the English more, especially for their trade and the homage they paid to him became a deciding factor in the French plans for his removal and the destruction of Pickawillany. Frenchmen were being murdered, trade goods stolen, alliances were shifting. It was time to end this threat, with a punitive expedition.

But how, and led by whom? In 1751, the year after English colors were raised by "Old Briton" over Pickawillany, a French force commanded by Sieur de Bellestre, accompanied by the Chevalier de Longueuil and Algonkin and Nipissing allies descended from Detroit. This force met with unexpected resistance on the part of the western allies of the French. This party led by Bellestre finally left Detroit with only seventeen Nipissing, and pushed on, but could no nothing with so small a force. They managed to kill and scalp two stragglers, but had to retreat to French territory without being able to destroy their objective.[7] After this embarrassment to French arms, Langlade, with approval and assistance from Céloron, vowed himself to lead a punitive force of French and Indians, and destroy Pickawillany once and for all.

> An evident talent for warfare and the influence of powerful relatives procured him a cadetship in La Marine. Burning to distinguish himself by some effort, on behalf of his country, he heard with shame of the several defeats at the post of Pickawillany. By some means Langlade succeeded in enlisting a force of over 240 savages, keen for French honor and fired by the enthusiasm of their youthful leader.[8]

By what savage rites young Langlade played upon his allies' minds we do not know. At a later time when attempting to raise a force among reluctant Indians, he resorted to the wild excitement of a dog feast to appeal to their savage bravery, and by this means succeeded. By some such legerdemain he aroused the martial vigor of his followers, and with the consent and blessing of the commandant at Detroit, marched against Pickawillany. The journal of this expedition has unfortunately been lost; we know of it only by the results reported, and by the accounts of the English traders. According to these latter sources it was a wild and horrid raid.[9]

In *The History of the Maumee River Basin* the raid is described as follows:

> A force of about two hundred and fifty Chippewas and Ottawas was gathered at the north and, led by Charles Langlade, were reinforced at Detroit by M. St. Ours [an ensign in les Compagnies Franches] with a few French regulars and Canadians, and all passed rapidly across Lake Erie, up the Maumee and St. Mary, and across the portage to Pickawillany where they attacked the town and fort early in the morning of 21 June, 1752. Most of the Aborigines were distant, and after a sharp battle, the town and fort were surrendered to the assailants. One Englishman was wounded, then stabbed and partly eaten. Five Englishmen were taken prisoners, and two, Thomas Burney and Andrew McBryer, escaped to tell the particulars. Fourteen Miamis were shot, including La Demoiselle, whom they boiled and ate. 'Seventy years of missionaries had not weaned them from cannibalism.'[10]

In *Century of Conflict*, author Joseph Lister Rutledge describes the scene from a somewhat different viewpoint:

> Two years after Céloron's return, a French trader of mixed birth from Green Bay named Charles de Langlade, followed somewhat the same route. His reasons were probably personal. The Demoiselle had disturbed the trading habits of the region in a way that Langlade could not approve. He gathered a force of Ojibways and Ottawas, who didn't need any specific reason, and led them against Pickawillany. Most of its male inhabitants were away on the hunt, and the attackers were unannounced, so the end was quick and complete. The victors prepared a great feast. Perhaps it is indelicate to

record that the chief dainty at that hilarious feast was nothing less than La Demoiselle himself. Broiled to the savage taste, he was eaten by the victors, who gave every evidence of a hearty appetite.[11]

In *Crucible of War*, author Fred Anderson not only gives a more graphic description of the raid, but also sums up the effects of it for all sides, British, French, and Indian.

At about nine o'clock on the morning of June 21, 1752, a party of about 180 Chippewa and 30 Ottawa warriors, accompanied by 30 French soldiers from Detroit under the command of a French-Ottawa officer names Charles-Michel de Langlade, attacked the settlement. Most of Pickawillany's men were away hunting; most of its women, who were working in the cornfields, were made captive. After a six-hour siege, Langlade called a cease-fire. He said he would return the women and spare the defenders (who numbered only about twenty) if they agreed to surrender the English traders. Lacking any alternative, the defenders agreed, then looked on while the raiders demonstrated what the consequences of trading with the English could be. First they dispatched a wounded trader 'and took out his heart and ate it;' then they turned their attention to the settlement's headman, Memeskia. This chief, known to the French as La Demoiselle, had lately acquired a new sobriquet, Old Briton, from the English trader Croghan and his colleagues. Now, to repay 'his attachment to the English' and to acquire his power for themselves, the raiders 'boiled him and ate him all up.' Then with five profoundly apprehensive traders and a vast quantity of booty in hand, they returned to Detroit. Behind them lay the smoking ruin that, twenty-four hours earlier, had been one of the largest settlements and the richest trading post west of the Appalachians.[12]

French prestige and power soared after this raid. The English thorn, so prevalent in the side of the French interests, had been quickly and permanently removed. So grateful was the Governor-General of Canada, that he bestowed a pension upon Langlade. Louise Phelps Kellogg, in her book, *The French Regime in Wisconsin and the Northwest*, sums it all up in these words:

> This act of war in time of peace had a profound influence on the affairs of both colonies. From this time forward until the latter years of the French and Indian War, the French controlled both the fur trade and the occupancy of the Ohio valley. The English fortunes declined. Most of the Miami returned to the Maumee; the site of Pickawillany became a desert. The valiant youth from Mackinac was pensioned by his government and entered the colonial army, in which he received the commission of an Ensign in 1755, and that of Lieutenant in 1760. From this event the inter-colonial rivalry entered upon a new phase.[13]

The legend of Langlade was on the rise.

The Monongahela 1755

The next important achievement of Charles-Michel de Langlade was in the battle fought over the lands that bordered La Belle Riviere (the beautiful river), which flowed through the Ohio valley and was claimed by both France and England.

Both sides knew the importance of the Ohio country and the rivers that flowed through it. Both were determined to seize the strategic ground and establish fortified posts, especially at the confluence of the Allegheny, Monongahela, and Ohio Rivers, known as "the Forks."

The French came down from the north "when Governor Duquesne decided to dispatch a large force of troops and milice to wrest control of the Ohio valley. He chose Marine officer Captain Paul Marin de la Malgue to lead and command it."[14]

Marin's orders were to establish posts or forts on the south shore of Lake Erie, all the way to the Forks. The first was Fort Presque Isle (today the site of Erie, Pennsylvania). This was accomplished in May of 1753, and further south, Fort le Boeuf was completed in July. Following that, the construction of Fort Machault, at the Indian village of Venango (today's Franklin, Pennsylvania) was completed. The herculean task of transporting the boats and supplies, the back-breaking labor of building the forts, and the oppressive, hot weather that had to be endured, took a heavy toll of fatigue and sickness on the French forces. In fact Marin, who drove himself just as hard as his men, succumbed to overexertion and died. He was replaced by Jacques Legardeur de Saint-Pierre, another experienced officer of les Compagnies Franches.[15]

Unfortunately for the French, the British got to the Forks first. Governor Dinwiddie of Virginia, who had previously sent the French a letter carried by a young man named George Washington, demanded their (the French) removal from the Ohio Valley immediately. When the French refused, Dinwiddie ordered the raising of a force of two hundred men under the command of Washington (now promoted to Lieutenant Colonel) to the Forks of the Ohio. Also commissioned as Captain of the Virginia militia was William Trent, with John Fraser as Lieutenant, and Edward Ward as Ensign.[16] The English started their construction of a fort at the forks of the Ohio in early February of 1754.

In late March of 1754 supplies began to run low and Trent, as senior officer, decided himself to go and secure them and reinforcements. He left Ensign Ward in charge of finishing and manning the small fort the English would call Fort Prince George.[17] The toehold completed, it looked like the English were here to stay, especially to the local Indians. This was to change abruptly.

In mid-April of 1754, shortly after the fort's completion, Ensign Ward looked out to see a French force of marines and milice, disembarking from their boats, and forming up on the shore under the command of Captain Claude-Pierre Pecaudy, Sieur de Contrecoeur and his second in command, Artillery Captain Francois Le Mercier.

The French, splendid in their white *justacorps*, arrayed themselves in ranks, and with eighteen cannon alongside, marched to within 150 yards of the English fort garrisoned by Ward and his men. Under a flag of truce, Captain Le Mercier bowed graciously to Ward, and politely demanded surrender of the fort and removal of the English force. If Ward would not comply, Le Mercier and his cannon would blow the fort to matchsticks and the English to Hell. Ward wisely chose discretion over valor.[18]

The French, ever gracious in peace and war, allowed the English to leave Fort Prince George with their honor and possessions. The French even treated and hosted Ward and his men to a splendid supper that evening. The next morning, the French sent Ward and his soldiers on their way, dismantled the small Fort Prince George and began laying out the lines for a bigger, stronger, more permanent fort. It would be called Fort Duquesne, in honor of the governor. As author Fred Anderson states in *Crucible of War*, in describing Fort Duquesne, "Apart from Detroit and Niagara, it would be the most impressive military installation in the interior of the continent. One look could tell the story; the French had come to stay."[19]

It is June of 1755. Fort Duquesne stands completed, established, garrisoned, and a definite threat to England. To remove this threat, a mighty British army, allied with Colonial American militia, is about to embark from Virginia, travel through Pennsylvania, and lay siege to Fort Duquesne on the Forks of the Ohio. Leading this massive army, which includes regular British troops of the line, the 44th and 48th Regiments of Foot, plus a train of artillery big enough to batter down the walls of Quebec, is Major General Edward Braddock of His Majesty's Coldstream Guards. On his staff is young George Washington, who is still smarting from the devastating defeat that the French dealt him at Fort Necessity a few months earlier.

Braddock's army is impressive, over 2000 men, staffed by many battle-hardened officers and troops, and generally regarded as unstoppable. In early June of 1755, this magnificent army started its slow, tedious, and inexorable march across the mountains. Beset with backbreaking labor, and great difficulty, this army finally neared its objective in early July 1755.

Captain Pierre de Contrecoeur, who was in charge of Fort Duquesne, was in a predicament, and was understandably nervous. The French had to stop, or TRY to stop, this juggernaut coming towards them, but how? Captain Contrecoeur's third in command was Captain Jean-Daniel Dumas, who was born in France and served as a lieutenant in the War of the Austrian Succession in Bavaria, Provence, and Italy. He arrived in Canada in 1750, and was a captain in the Compagnies Franches de la Marine. Second in command, and due to replace Contrecoeur, was Captain Daniel-Hyacinthe Marie-Lienard de Beaujeu. This man was no slouch, either, when it came to battle experience. In June of 1746, then-Lt. Beaujeu was one of the leaders of a French force sent to Nova Scotia, to link up with other French forces and try to recapture Fortress Louisbourg, which had surrendered to English and American forces in 1745. Beaujeu's journal of the ten-month campaign includes detailed accounts of their greatest exploit. After a 150-mile march in bitter mid-winter, Beaujeu's force of 300 French and Indians attacked 500 New Englanders billeted in Grand Pré, and forced their surrender after a bloody fight.[20]

So Contrecoeur had a small force of tough French troops, battle-hardened officers, some Canadian milice, and a sizeable contingent of French-allied Indians. And Ensign Charles-Michel de Langlade, who had led a very sizeable force of Ottawas, Chippewas, and others from the Great Lakes region, stood out as their brother, father, and leader. When Contrecoeur, Beaujeu, and Dumas convened to discuss strategy, it is almost certain that Langlade would have been there too. While Dumas, Beaujeu, and Contrecoeur were all French Marine officers, and were experienced and familiar with commanding and dealing with Indians, Langlade was ONE of them. He could understand them and speak for them better than any other French officer.

History tells of the French decision to fight Braddock's army before it got within siege range of Fort Duquesne. The Indians, however, were not in agreement. They had seen the size and strength of Braddock's army, and considered fighting it tantamount to suicide. It was up to the French partisan leaders to convince them otherwise. On the morning of July 8, 1755, Captain Daniel de Beaujeu appeared before the assembled tribes, bare-chested, "stripped to the waist, his

gorget alone marking him as a French officer."[21] He knelt and
received communion from Father Denys, and then went to
address the Indian allies. With him was the French force
similarly dressed, as Edward P. Hamilton, former Director of
Fort Ticonderoga, states, "most of the force, and certainly the
officers, were in Indian dress."[22]

Beaujeu appears to have argued, harangued, cajoled,
insulted, and finally convinced the Indians to come and fight
alongside of the French. Undoubtedly, Langlade was also
there and played the same role. After setting the Indians'
bloodthirst on fire, and handing out great quantities of
powder and ball, the combined French force headed out of
Fort Duquesne to meet the British. It totaled 36 officers and 72
soldiers of *les troupes de la marine*, 146 milice, and 637 Indians.

> The Indian group included a few Mingos and Delawares,
> and a somewhat larger contingent of Shawnees, but was
> mostly composed of French allies from the North and
> West—Ottawas, Mississaugas, Wyandots, Potawatomies—
> lured by the prospect of captives and booty. Among the
> leaders of the Far Indians was Charles Langlade, that
> tough and experienced officer who had destroyed
> Pickawillany in 1752. The party, well armed but otherwise
> unburdened by supplies and equipment, set out from the
> fort about nine in the morning, intending to ambush
> Braddock's column.[23]

Unbelievably, unexpectedly, unexplainably, the two
opposing forced collided together. Both were surprised. The
British, gaining their senses more quickly, formed to the front,
and started to fire in volleys. The French regulars, under
Beaujeu's commands, did likewise. Unfortunately, with the
third volley from the English muskets, Beaujeu was killed
instantly. The French Indians began to waver and, had it
ended then, history would have been re-written.

BRADDOCK'S DEFEAT, JULY 9, 1755
From an oil painting by Edwin Willard Deming

But somehow the French rallied. Accounts differ, but generally Dumas is given the credit. He writes in his report:

> It was then, by word and gesture, I sought to rally the few soldiers who remained. I advanced, with an assurance born of despair. My platoon gave forth a withering fire which astonished the enemy. It grew imperceptibly, and the Indians, seeing that my attack had caused the enemy to stop shouting, returned to me.[24]

While Dumas and his French marines held their ground (a lot of the milice had run away), Langlade and the Indian chiefs saw a golden opportunity. Immediately they led their followers along the flanks of the British column, taking cover behind trees and rocks, and pouring a murderous barrage into the redcoats clustered in the wooded road below them. Frightened at this new development, the forward British units attempted to retreat, only to collide with their own advancing regiments. Hearing the sounds of battle, Braddock and his men charged to the front. What then resulted was described as a collapsing telescope, and units became horribly mixed and tangled. British officers, trying to untangle this mess, evident by their shouts, dress, and bearing, offered special targets for French marksmanship, and they were cut down in droves. The British regulars, now leaderless, unable to return fire at an unseen enemy, began to panic and huddled in a mass for protection. To the French and Indians it became a turkey shoot, every lead ball found a victim, sometimes two. After three hours of this, the army that could not go forward had to go back. Braddock, foreseeing imminent encirclement and destruction, ordered retreat. Immediately he suffered a wound, knocking him from his horse, and which would later prove mortal.

Any semblance of order now evaporated and the British began a headlong rush to the rear, back to the ford of the river, in uncontrollable panic. The French and Indians gave up the pursuit at the water's edge. They then returned to finish off the wounded, take prisoners, and collect immense heaps of booty. It has been called "Braddock's Defeat." It should have been called a massacre.

While Dumas, as the senior surviving officer, received the credit for the victory, who rallied the Indians? Contrecoeur was in Fort Duquesne, Beaujeu was dead, and Dumas made his gallant stand with the French marines. History suggests strongly that it could have been, must have been, Langlade. Kopperman states in his book, *Braddock on the Monongahela*, that the final credit for the success of the French ambuscade must go to Dumas, Langlade, or both. There was plenty of glory to go around. In *La Corne St. Luc – His Flame*, authors Burnham and Martin quote a letter of over 20 years later, written by General John Burgoyne during the Revolutionary War, which states, "I am informed that the Ottawas and other remote nations who are now within two days of joining me are more warlike and less rapacious. They are besides under the conduct of two of the ablest partisans of the last war – St. Luc, a Canadian gentleman, and one Langlade, THE very man who projected and executed with these very nations, the defeat of General Braddock."[25]

Langlade's fame is still in its ascendancy.

❧ *Lac Champlain et Lac du St. Sacrement 1756*

From the available records, we know that, after leading his warriors home after Braddock's defeat, Langlade returned to the East in August of 1756 where he and his Indians were employed as scouts for Fort Duquesne.[26]

The 1757 Battle on Snowshoes—Langlade's Ambush.

A letter written by the Marquis de Montcalm, on December 31, 1756 states, "M. Langlade, half-pay Ensign of the Colony troops, has left this morning with a detachment of fifty Canadians and Indians to go to Carillon, and from there to go on a party to Fort George (William Henry) and Fort Lydius (Edward)."[27]

When Langlade and his Indians arrived at Carillon, they reported to the commandant, Captain Paul-Louis Lusignan, of les Compagnies Franches de la Marine.[28] Here they rested from their travels, and were outfitted and supplied in preparation for their scouts and raids. The action they were seeking would not be long in coming.

Sometime in January, 1757, Robert Rogers received the same type of scouting orders from his superiors.[29] Leading a group of Rangers north from Fort Edward on January 15, Rogers arrived at Fort William Henry at dusk and spent the next two days, as did Langlade, outfitting his men in preparation of a winter scout. Here is the scene as painted by the master, Francis Parkman:

> Major Eyre and his soldiers, in their wilderness exile by the borders of Lake George, wiled the winter away with few other excitements than the evening howl of wolves from the frozen mountains, or some nocturnal savage shooting at a sentinel from behind a stump on the moonlit fields of snow. A livelier incident at last broke the monotony of their lives. In the middle of January Rogers came with his Rangers from Fort Edward, bound on a scouting party towards Crown Point. They spent two days at Fort William Henry in making snowshoes and other preparations, and set out on the seventeenth. They marched down the frozen lake and encamped at the Narrows. Some of them, unaccustomed to snowshoes, had become unfit for travel, and were sent back, thus reducing the number to seventy-four. In the morning they marched

again, by icicled rocks and icebound waterfalls, mountains grey with naked woods and fir-trees bowed down with snow. They passed Ticonderoga undiscovered, and stopped at night some five miles beyond it. The weather was changing, and rain was coming in. They scraped away the snow with their snowshoes, piled it in a bank around them, made beds of spruce-boughs, built fires, and lay down to sleep while the sentinels kept watch in the outer gloom. In the morning there was a drizzling rain, and the softened snow stuck to their snowshoes. They marched eastward three miles through the dripping forest, till they reached the banks of Lake Champlain, near what is now called Five Mile Point, and presently saw a sledge, drawn by horses, moving on the ice from Ticonderoga towards Crown Point. Rogers sent Lt. John Stark along the shore to the left to head it off, while he with another party, covered by woods, moved in the opposite direction to stop its retreat. He soon saw eight or ten more sledges following the first, and sent a messenger to prevent Stark from showing himself too soon; but Stark was already on the ice. All the sledges turned back in hot haste. The Rangers ran in pursuit and captured three of them, with seven men and six horses, while the rest escaped to Ticonderoga. The prisoners being separately examined, told an ominous tale. There were 350 regulars at Ticonderoga; 200 Canadians and 45 Indians had lately arrived there, and more Indians were expected that evening,—all destined to waylay the communications between the English forts, and all prepared to march at a moment's notice. The Rangers were now in great peril. The fugitives would give warning of their presence, and the French and Indians, in overwhelming force, would no doubt cut off their retreat."[30]

Abenaki Warrior.
(Illustration by George "Peskunck" Larrabee.)

The scene must have played out something like this:

"At approximately 11:30 a.m. Captain Lusignan was busy in his officer's room at Carillon, when he heard the shouts and clamor of men outside on the parade ground. Opening the door, he saw through the misty rain a steaming, panting horse covered with mud and snow, obviously ridden hard. Its rider was already bounding toward him, flushed with excitement.

Quickly and breathlessly, the courier recounted the startling events to Lusignan. There had been an ambush of the sleigh detail, about halfway to Fort St. Frederic, by about 100 English Rangers. Close behind the courier came the rest of the sleighs, led by DeRouilly, the officer in charge of the detail,[31] who corroborated the soldier's account.

Captain Lusignan promptly ordered his officers to assemble and meet in his quarters. In that crowded room hurried choices and decisions were made. Since the Rangers had attacked the convoy from the western shore, it stood to reason that their route of travel had been north and west of Carillon, probably following the *Route des Agniers*, or Mohawk trail, through the mountain valley west of the French posts. The Rangers could have crossed the lake and returned down the east side of it after the ambush, but that was thought unlikely. If they did, it would be almost impossible to plot their course and set an ambush.

However, if they were foolish enough to return upon their same outgoing trail, perhaps it could be found in time to catch them in an ambush. It was Lusignan's best — and probably — his only choice.

Studying the room carefully, his eyes quickly fell upon the kind of leader equal to the woodsmanship of the rangers: Ensign Charles-Michel Mouet de Langlade of les Compagnies Franches de la Marine, who had arrived in

December at the head of approximately 90 Chippewa and Ottawa warriors. Langlade was already the stuff legends were made of in *la petit guerre,* the savage, no-holds-barred war of the forests."[32]

Langlade quickly assembled his force of Indians and Canadians and headed west to the valley known today as Trout Brook. Here, some three miles southwest of Carillon, they found the prints made by the snowshoes of Rogers and his men. Following them northward, they came upon a ravine that was perfectly suited for their killing ground. While most stayed in cover behind the trees, silent as the gloomy woods itself, some went back to find and guide the bulk of the French regulars to the ambush site. The regulars, struggling along bravely and breathlessly through the knee-deep snow, were at a huge disadvantage; they were not equipped or familiar with snowshoes.[33] While Langlade and his Canadian and Indian force may have had their fusils protected from the rain by greased leather lock covers and wooden tompions, the regular troops from France did not, hence their fusils, which had been carried through the hours of rain and waist-deep snow, were in effect being rendered useless. On the other hand, Robert Rogers and his Rangers had the foresight to return to the campfires of their January 20 bivouac, rekindle the fires, and take the time to clean, dry, and re-load their muskets with fresh charges.[34]

It was about two or three o'clock on that dismal, rainy, overcast day in January, that the two forces came together. Rogers disregarded the advice of his men and decided to go back on his same path, contrary to his later famous "Rules for Ranging."[35]

The Rangers came back through the Trout Brook valley, on their tracks, in single files. Rogers himself was close to the front, and it has been stated that the English, in their cockiness, were actually singing as they marched![36] Whatever the noise, or lack of it, from the English column, the French were poised and ready. After descending a steep hill, crossing a ravine, and starting up another hill, the Rangers came face to face with Langlade and his troops, and a roar of muskets commenced.

Unfortunately for the French, many fusils did not go off, many misfired, and many hang-fired. A few of the lead Rangers were hit; some were killed, and others were wounded. Rogers, whose luck was always good in battle, was one of these, sustaining a glancing blow to his head. One has to wonder now, if the weather was dry, and if the aim was truer, or if that French fusil hadn't hang-fired, Robert Rogers and the later legends that accompanied him throughout life, might have ended right then and there.

Speculation aside, it became quite a firefight and lasted quite a while. Rogers and the lead elements turned, and under the covering fire of Lt. John Stark, made it back to the crest of the higher hill. But not all.

> Lieutenant Kennedy and a man named Gardiner were killed outright, along with several others. The French, exasperated by the deplorable misfiring of their weapons, bolted out of cover and, raising hue and cry, plunged through the snow to attack with fixed bayonets. Some of the wounded and slower Rangers met their demise at the point of cold steel.[37]
>
> M. de Lusignan at once sent off one hundred men of the regulars and colony troops, along with a few Indians and Canadian volunteers under the orders of M. de Basserode, captain of Languedoc, and M. d'Astral, lieutenant in the same regiment. M. de la Granville, captain in the regiment of La Reine, asked leave to go along as a volunteer. M. de Langlade, half-pay ensign of la Marine, was at the head of the Indians, almost all Ottawas.

The detachment went to lay an ambush on the road of the English, whose advanced guard appeared three hours after midday. After one discharge of musketry, which did not have the effect that one would expect, the rain which had been falling all day having wet the guns, our troops pounced upon the enemy with the bayonet and overwhelmed them. Their rear guard gained a height which overlooked that upon which our people were. They shot it out until nightfall, when the English seized the opportunity to retire in disorder."[38]

The battle pretty much ended in a draw — a stalemate, if you will. Neither side could dislodge the other, neither was willing to make a concentrated assault; the unwritten laws of *la petit guerre* would never allow that. Instead, the woodsmen of both sides hid behind rocks, trees, and blowdowns, sniping at each other until dusk closed in, followed quickly by darkness. Rogers and his officers made the right decision, to get out of there as quickly as possible. Cuneo says, "It was the first large-scale engagement in which Rogers had participated. Undoubtedly he aged during these few days in a way that only the leaders of small combat units can comprehend: for the first time he had failed to bring back all of his men."[39] Not only had he failed to bring back all of his men, in his haste to get away he inadvertently abandoned some of his wounded men. This was never forgotten and the horrors and sufferings of captivity, recorded by Private Thomas Brown in his journal, let others know that it would never be forgiven.[40]

While neither Langlade nor Rogers could claim clear-cut victory from this battle, it enhanced both of their reputations. They would face each other again and one day would meet at a far off post called Michilimackinac.

Two months later, in March of 1757, Pierre Rigaud de Vaudreuil, brother of Canadian Governor-General Marquis de Vaudreuil, and just as inept, led an abortive winter attack on Fort William Henry. Lacking surprise, and unable to muster the courage for an assault on the vastly outnumbered defenders, Rigaud had to settle for burning and destroying much of the fort's outbuildings and shipping, which included numerous bateaux and whaleboats.

Rigaud should have done much better. His force numbered over 1600 men: French regulars, Canadians, and Indians.[41] Bougainville states:

> The detachment of sixteen hundred men left (Carillon) on the fifteenth and camped on the right of Lac St. Sacrement, opposite M. de Contrecoeur's old camp. On the sixteenth at daybreak they sent off a scouting party of seventy-five Indians and twenty-five Frenchmen commanded by MM. de Hertel and St. Simon. The detachment proceeded down the middle of the lake in five columns, those of the right and the left composed of Indians commanded by MM. de Longueuil, father and son.[42]

Later entries mention other noted leaders such as Dumas, Langy, and St. Ours. But Langlade's name is not mentioned. Was he there and his presence not recorded? Or was he somewhere else? Since it is now March, and in two more months his name re-appears in journal entries, it is probable that he stayed in the Lac Champlain-Lac du St. Sacrement region leading small raids and ambushes.

We do know that in July and August, prior to the siege and destruction of Fort William Henry, Langlade sprang one of his most famous and devastating ambushes, one that took the lives of almost as many Englishmen as in the actual siege and "massacre" of Fort William Henry.

The ambush was forever known as "Sabbath Day Point."

❀ Sabbath Day Point

The Historical Legacy of Fred LaPann

This section is dedicated to our beloved and sorely missed friend, Fred LaPann.

The Battle on Snowshoes was the tie that bound Fred and me. Shortly after reading it, Fred called me on the telephone and wrote a subsequent letter. I still have it and along with his others, they are some of my most prized possessions. The Battle at Sabbath Day Point, like the Battle on Snowshoes, has been mentioned in history books, but was never fully developed or explored. Hopefully, this chapter will change that.

Fred was one of, if not *the*, greatest students of history that I have ever known. His knowledge came not only from the sources, journals, and book knowledge that we all have access to, but also from actual hands-on experience he acquired by living and exploring his whole life in those lands that we read about.

Fred lived all of his life in the Ticonderoga-Champlain valley. As a kid he went exploring the lakes, the mountains, the valleys, and the islands. His house, on Hague Road, faced the southwest slope of Rogers Rock. He spent more time up there than anyone I have ever known.

In May we would sit on his front porch and could see, imagine, Father Isaac Jogues being canoed into captivity by the Iroquois. In July we could see Montcalm's army passing by on its way to attack Fort William Henry; or the great armada of Abercromby, sailing in 1758 toward the death of Lord Howe and the devastation of the Black Watch Highlanders and the rest of his army at the log wall of

Montcalm. Under the blaze of autumn we could picture the scouts of partisans and Indians in their birchbark canoes, and Rangers in their whaleboats. As the lake became covered with ice we could visualize the winter expeditions of Courcelles and Rigaud de Vaudreuil, and the scouts and subsequent retreats of Rogers' Rangers after their crushing defeat by Langy and Durantaye at the Battle on Snowshoes. Where Fred had lived, history had passed by his porch.

But Fred was not one to sit idly upon the porch. He was constantly exploring, seeking, searching. The knowledge that he passed on to me, I in turn share with you, the reader, reenactor, and lover of history.

Fred took me and showed me the exact location of the French daily patrol trail. He took me over the *Route des Agniers*, where de Lévis marched the land force of Montcalm's army in 1757 to their rendezvous at Northwest Bay. We went to Isle au Mouton, Isle la Barque, and Sabbath Day Point. We meticulously scoured all the trails and ravines of Mt. Pélée (Rogers Rock). He showed me the only two possible escape routes for Robert Rogers and his wounded Rangers after their defeat at the Battle on Snowshoes. (And neither one was the much fabled "Slide.") I observed first hand the entrance to the Trout Brook valley from Friends Point through Swingers Notch. We visited many times the actual crossing spot of Trout Brook that figured so prominently in Rogers snowshoe fights and the destination of Langy and Trépezec on that fateful day of July 6, 1758, where Lord Howe met his demise. We trekked over the route of Cooks and Bear Mountains, which we believe Langy and Trépezec's force followed that day, and we have been on Bulwagga Mountain and stood where Rogers made his observations of Fort St. Frederic at present-day Crown Point.

Fred was a wonderful son, brother, husband, and father. He was a superb guidance counselor to troubled teenagers. He was an avid hunter, outdoorsman, and conservationist. He was a marathon runner, a history buff, and an incredible friend to all who knew him. He was one in a million. Life without him won't be the same for Holly and me.

Fred, this one's for you.

❧ *July 1757*

Charles-Michel de Langlade stood on the point that evening. At his feet, the clear blue waters of Lac St. Sacrement lapped gently against the sandy shore. The fall of evening was upon him, and the strong scent of the pines was being wafted towards him on a gentle west wind. He had selected this ambush spot two days ago in council with the Ottawa and Chippewa chiefs, and it was considered ideal for its purpose. This point, which jutted far out into the lake, was a perfect site to easily land, launch, and conceal canoes. It had plenty of area and was flat, with tall grasses and more sand than rocks on its shore. Farther back, among the towering pines, was room to conceal the hundreds of warriors that were now encamped there.

As he stood there in the evening shadows, he reflected upon the past tumultuous weeks spent at Carillon. Never in his young life had he witnessed such a powerful military force assembled for New France. The Marquis de Montcalm had gathered his troupes de la terre, Compagnies Franches de la Marines, and milice units, the total of which must have numbered above six thousand men.

But what staggered the mind even more was the assemblage of Indians; not just the traditional French Christianized ones like the Abenakis, Algonquins, Crees and Nipissings, but Indians from the far west, some of whom could not converse in French or any known tongue, and with whom the interpreters had to resort to the use of sign language for communication. Langlade himself had led a large band of Ottawa and Chippewa warriors to Carillon from the Great Lakes.

In the days and weeks previous, scouting parties of Indians and French officers had ebbed and flowed from Carillon on raids to the south. When not in the field, these men would spend much time talking, trading, and in council. As young warriors have always done since the beginning of time, stories of raids, ambushes, and hunts were shared. Along with these Indians of various tribes, were men like himself, French partisan leaders. Some he knew; some he knew of, some he did not.

Langlade had recognized Saint-Luc de La Corne, whom Montcalm had personally chosen as "General" over all the Indians and their partisan leaders. He knew the wild and reckless Joseph Marin, who, like his father Paul, had been at various posts throughout the Great Lakes region. He liked Marin, as well as Ensign de Corbiére, who had just reinforced him this evening with 450 more French and Indians. Others were there too, like Niverville, Sabrevois, Fleurimont, La Plante and Hertel.

One partisan leader whom he had taken exceptional liking to, and from whom he felt a strong return, was Langis de Montegron, an Ensign in the Compagnies Franches like himself. Although Langis was nearly five years older, Langis and Langlade got along fabulously, like brothers. Langis had heard of Langlade's exploits such as the raid and destruction of Pickawillany, and the stunning defeat of Braddock's army on the banks of the Monongahela. Langlade in turn had heard of Langis, the favorite of Montcalm, and liked to listen to Langis tell of his parts in the sieges of Fort Beausejour and Oswego, and this past winter's abortive attack on Fort William Henry under the inept command of Rigaud de Vaudreuil.

But the favorite topic of conversation between them was the recently formed companies of English Rangers under the command of their captain, Robert Rogers, who were turning out to be quite worthy adversaries in the forest. Langlade shared with Langis his ideas, feelings, and experiences with this unconventional group. They were good and getting better at *la petit guerre*. Rogers, the leader, was young, tough, and fearless, but he still had a lot to learn. Langlade told of this past January, when Rogers and his Rangers had ambushed the provision sleighs going from Carillon to St. Frederic, capturing three and taking seven soldiers prisoner. The remainder of the French convoy whirled around and made it back to the safety of Carillon, where they told the commandant, Lusignan, what had happened. Lusignan assembled a force of volunteer soldiers and sent Langlade and his Indians to try and find the Rangers' trail. That part was easy, Langlade told Langis. Rogers and his 74 Rangers had snowshoed north along the *Route des Agniers* towards St. Frederic, and had left a well-packed trail. Finding an ambush spot was also easy; a narrow defile between two hills that blocked the way home for the English. The problem was the weather extremely damp and rainy, and the soldiers from the fort were not equipped with *raquettes*, making travel and maneuver difficult.

Rogers and his Rangers soon were seen coming back on their trail leading southward, and when in range the ambush was sprung. Unfortunately, the moisture of the day had rendered many of the French fusils useless, and a good part of the Ranger casualties were from tomahawk and bayonet. The battle became a sniping action throughout the afternoon, until darkness ended the stalemate, and Rogers and his survivors slipped safely away in the night. Langlade felt that Rogers was lucky; perhaps he led a charmed life. It was certain that a lot of his men were not so fortunate. Langlade also wondered if Rogers was careless, or just cocky, in his mistake of returning the same way he had come. The story seemed to intrigue Langis, and he kept it in his mind for future use. Perhaps someday he would meet this Rogers and his Rangers in battle. It paid to know your enemy's traits in the savage war of the forest.

A movement to his front brought Langlade out of his reverie. Gliding ghostlike out of the dusk came two birchbark canoes of Chippewa warriors. They told Langlade of seeing a number of English boats anchoring for the night near some islands, towards the eastern mountains.

The cry of a loon brought the force of French and Indians out of the woods like an apparition. There on the point, with muted voices, a council was convened and a strategy decided. The decision was made to lie in wait here, on the point, instead of trying to seek out and attack the English. Perhaps, with any luck, the English boats would proceed northward along this shore tomorrow. Given that chance, perhaps an ambush could be sprung. This was the Indian way; to lie in wait, and use stealth and concealment to trap your prey. Perhaps they could create a ruse, or decoy the boats into coming into range. They would wait and see what the morning would bring.

Langlade, like his warriors, had slept uneasily through the night. The possibility of a battle kept them taut and their dreams disturbed. The night was exceptionally cool and the dampness had a slight chill to it.

Near the islands, where he had anchored for the night, Col. John Parker and his officers were coming awake after a fitful night's rest. Colonel Parker and his "Jersey Blues" were crowded aboard 20 whaleboats and two bay boats with sail. They were on a reconnaissance in force from Fort William Henry, sent out by Col. George Monro. Their mission was to take prisoners, perhaps fire the sawmill and advanced posts, and most importantly, to find out what the Marquis de Montcalm was up to. Previous scouting parties of Rangers, Mohawks, and provincials had had little or no success. Embarrassingly enough, just a few days before, an ambush was set by over 100 English on the shore of Isle la Barque, for the daily French reconnaissance barge that prowled the northern waters of the lake. Outnumbered ten to one, the men on the French barge fought their way out of the trap at a cost of one cadet killed and three wounded. The English could not catch up with the fast French vessel. This kind of shameful action would not happen to his force of 350, Parker thought. He was now in charge of perhaps the greatest flotilla of English boats even seen on Lake George and he was going to make its presence felt to the French. Stocked with five companies of New Jersey provincials, it should be enough, Parker thought, to outnumber and overpower any French or Indian force on the lake.

Colonel Parker was dead wrong.

Exercising caution, Parker and his officers decided to use the heavy morning mist as cover. Parker ordered three of the whaleboats to scout the western shore northwards, while three others would follow behind in support at a discreet distance. Finally, the whole of the flotilla would follow.

The same mist that Parker counted on as cover, was also his undoing. Out of that mist, powered by the arms and shoulders of some of his Canadians, shot a birchbark canoe, heading to the tip of the point where Langlade stood. Whistling the signal call of the white-throated sparrow, Langlade stepped to the shore to hear their report; English boats were following, heading straight towards the point. Langlade whirled around intending to alert the camp, but found to his surprise the entire force standing silent and motionless behind him. At the chief's signal, the Ottawas and Chippewas raced back to the cover of the pines and took their places alongside their canoes. Lying in the tall grass, Langlade turned his head to the left and saw the "ruse" being readied. Some Canadians had dressed in the clothing of English provincials, which had been procured from some captured soldiers of a party commanded by a Captain West from Fort Edward. Standing next to them were some Chippewa warriors with red flags of cloth in their hands. The red flags, carried by the French Indians were also intended to confuse and mollify the English. This, Langlade and de Corbiére had learned from captured dispatches of West's patrol, was supposed to identify these Indians as "friendly" to any English troops. Behind the Canadians and "friendly" Indians, lay the real force; concealed, guns at the ready.[43]

Turning his head, Langlade strained his eyes, trying to pierce the misty fog, which lay upon the water like a wraith. Suddenly, like a dream, whaleboats appeared, gliding over the surface, not 100 yards from the shore. He could hear muted voices and coughs and the bumping of oars, carried across the stillness of the lake. The boats continued onward and suddenly a sharp command was given. Langlade tensed as the moment of truth approached, but unbelievably, the English took the bait, believing that this was Captain West's force of scouts and friendly Indians, and swung into shore. As soon as the boats ran aground, the hidden force of French and Ottawas sprang up, fusils at the ready. The English were taken prisoners without a shot being fired. As Langlade watched, more noises from the lake brought his attention back to the front. Another three whaleboats glided past, following the course of their brothers, and as they rowed northward, they noticed the lead boats drawn up on the shore. Rowing in to investigate what their comrades had found, they too were captured. "Incredible!" thought Langlade, as his nerves shook with excitement.

Turning his head back to the front, Langlade saw and heard at the same time, Parker's main force of boats coming by. Parker and his men never glanced at the point; instead, their loud voices told Langlade that Parker had just noticed his six boats drawn up on shore and was speeding up to see what the matter was. Langlade rolled over on his back and glanced to his rear. What he saw reminded him of a panther. The Indians, silent, crouched, hands on their canoes, only moving their dark eyes. Suddenly, shouts from the boats and a scattering of shots told the fact that the trap had somehow been sprung. Instantly, as one gigantic mass, the force of French, Ottawas, and Chippewas rose up, rushed to the water with their canoes, and made the water froth with the strokes of their paddles. Their speed and momentum carried them swiftly around the point, and they sped towards Parker, whose boats were stopped and whose attention was focused on the firing coming from the French and Indians on the shore. The English never saw the canoes coming until they were upon them with the tomahawk and war cry.

Parker's Jersey Blues on Lake George.
(Illustration by Ralph Mitchard.)

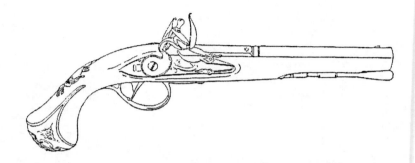

This is one of a pair of English flintlock pistols formerly owned by Charles de Langlade in Wisconsin. This moderately decorated piece is of excellent workmanship and beautiful balance, and is in good taste throughout. It and its mate were made by Bate of London, presumably about 1775 or earlier. This pistol is a fair example of the hand weapons of the aristocrats of the period. Behind the cock is a safety bolt which permits the piece to be locked in half-cock position, a safety provision which came into general use in the last half of the eighteenth century. Nicely worked silver ornaments the grip. The half-octagon barrel and the lock plate of iron are marked with modest decorations. The smooth bore of approximately .60 caliber permits a load with real stopping power. The weapon is at once befitting the dignity of a leader and equal to practical demands that might be placed upon it.

— *Guns on the Early Frontiers* by Carl P. Russell, pp. 84-86.
Bonanza Books, New York.

Their avenue of retreat to the rear being blocked, caught in a murderous crossfire, Parker and his men panicked. They had never imagined a force bigger than theirs could be on the lake. Parker and four of his boats turned east, rowing and firing desperately, and managed to free themselves from the jaws of death. Most of his force was not so lucky: over 280 were killed or taken prisoner out of the total English force of 350.[44]

The Indians on the shore had fired a deadly barrage, killing and wounding many. Other Indians in canoes had come up to the boats, and grabbing the sides, jumped into the water overturning them. Many English were drowned; others were speared like fish. Some of the Jersey Blues swam ashore and tried to make a run for it. Langlade watched as the Indians ran them down as a wolf does a deer.

Finally, it was all over but the shouting, and there was plenty of that. If the blood lust and excitement of the battle were not enough, the rum found in the whaleboats was greedily quaffed, and the Ottawas went over the edge. Fires were started, three of the Jersey Blues were dismembered and put in the pot, fulfilling their promise to Montcalm to eat the meat (flesh) of the English, and drink the broth (blood).[45]

Langlade and de Corbiére walked wearily a discreet distance away. Killing was one thing, cannibalism was quite another. However, both knew better than to chide or reproach their ferocious allies.

Parker's frightened survivors arrived at Fort William Henry a few days later and the message they brought was terrifying. The French had unleashed the Indians. Hell would follow shortly.

How much of the Sabbath Day Point chapter is true? How much is fiction? Basically, all of it is true. The dates, times, numbers, and participants such as Parker, West, Langlade and Corbiére are all documented in the history books.

I have taken the writer's privilege of working all of those facts into a story, much like Allan Eckert did in *Wilderness Empire.*

It cannot be proven beyond a shadow of a doubt that the stratagem of red flags was what actually lured Parker's first six bateaux into the trap. Neither can it be disproved. In lieu of any other evidence, it is possible and very probable.

Bougainville's journal entry of July 22, 1757 states:

> Various papers have been found while following the trail of the fugitives, among which are the instructions given by General Webb to the officer commanding this party of twenty men, detached from [Captain] West's company of volunteers. By these instructions it would appear that the English are maintaining scouts at the foot of the bay all the time, that their post is behind the rocks alongside of which M. de Langlade was fired at. They remained in ambush there for two days. Their orders are to observe the French detachments which pass in this region, to attack them if they are weak enough, and, if they are too strong, not to reveal themselves but to send a man to Fort Edward to warn them of the road the French took. They were cautioned that friendly Indians will come to them with a red flag in hand, that they will give them the password, which is Johnson, and will show them a passport signed William.[46]

Given that knowledge, it would have been the logical bait to employ.

1759

Montmorency River

The Dictionary of Canadian Biography briefly states "Langlade was present at the siege of Quebec two years later. If the reinforcements he had requested of Lévis had arrived in time, he and his Indians might have destroyed the detachment Wolfe took to reconnoiter up the Montmorency River on 26 July, 1759. Instead, both sides withdrew after a brief skirmish."[47]

A better picture is painted by author Gordon Donaldson in his book, *Battle for a Continent*:

On July 26, Wolfe took Murray with 2000 men up the east bank of the Montmorency, looking for the ford that Chevalier Johnstone had found for the French three weeks before. They discovered it and camped for the night in the forest by the rippling shallows. As the troops wandered about from tent to tent, gambling and swapping boasts and stories, they did not know that 800 Indians under Charles de Langlade were lying motionless, tomahawks in hand, less than a hundred yards away. They lay there for five hours while Langlade hurried to de Lévis' camp to announce another fine opportunity to slaughter the English. Again, de Lévis sent for permission to attack and none came. And again the Indians grew tired of waiting. At dawn they rose and swooped down on Wolfe's regulars, killing and wounding 150, driving them *and* General Wolfe in headlong retreat to their camp. Wolfe roused Brigadier Townshend's entire brigade and sent Brigadier Murray back to counterattack at the ford. Although the Indians were driven back across the river, along with a detachment of Canadians who had come to support them, Murray lost another forty-five men and came back in a hurry. It was Wolfe's first defeat; worse, he had been beaten by a tribe of savages and a pack of Canadian dogs."[48]

Allan Eckert, in the well-researched *Wilderness Empire,* places Langlade and Pontiac, both favorites of Montcalm, together in the forest glades lining the banks of the Montmorency.

Another aggressive move by Wolfe resulted in the landing of three thousand troops just below the mouth of the Montmorenci River, where they established an encampment. Four hundred of Pontiac's Indians, being led by the war chief and Charles Langlade, discovered them first, while the [English] attackers were still in a state of unpreparedness. While his Indians lay in hiding, watching them, Langlade hastened to the nearby encampment of eleven hundred Canadians under Captain Repentigny with a request for support for an immediate attack. Unwilling to act on his own, Repentigny sent a runner with the intelligence to General Lévis to ask for orders. Lévis, in turn had been specifically ordered by Vaudreuil to inform him of all moves without fail *before* they were made, and so now he relayed the message and request upon the governor, whose headquarters were about four miles away. Vaudreuil kept them waiting two hours, and the Indians, impatient at best, finally launched the attack by themselves. They struck Wolfe's unit hard, inflicting heavy losses and forcing it back until, at last, steadied by the rangers, the English force held its ground and broke up the attack. In their retreat, the Indians picked up thirty-nine scalps of Wolfe's men.

Massacre at Montmorency. (Illustration by Joe Lee.)

Langlade, furious for lack of support, which he felt could have delivered a decisively crippling blow to the enemy rather than just a painful one, was almost ready to throw down his weapons and leave with his Chippewa Indians. He was stopped by Pontiac.

'You will not go, and they will not go,' the war chief told him. 'I have given my word to the little general [Montcalm] that I will fight beside him as long as there is breath left in him, or in me, and I will live by my word or die by it.'[49]

All of these writings make me wonder, and, at the same time know, that if the Canadian Governor Vaudreuil had not been such a pompous, snooty, incompetent buffoon, and if he had allowed his fighting men such as de Lévis and Langlade to make on-the-spot decisions, history could have been, *would* have been different.

If the French and Indian force could have swept across the river at the right moment, such as dusk or dawn, a catastrophe, like that of Braddock's Defeat, would have taken place. Here were hundreds of British regulars, grouped together in a thick, primeval forest, with General Wolfe in the midst, being attacked by French and Indians by none other than Charles-Michel de Langlade, the same victor over Braddock! Talk about *deja vu*! If Wolfe had been killed or captured, which was very possible, then there would not ever have been the classic battle on the Plains of Abraham, and Quebec, and New France, would have survived for yet another year.

❧ Quebec 1759

But, alas, it was not meant to be. James Wolfe did live to attack Quebec on September 13, 1759, and on that fateful day, both he and Montcalm suffered mortal wounds. Montcalm was brought to the Surgeon Arnoux's house, after bringing his shattered regiments back through the St. Louis Gate. Allan Eckert, more than any other writer that I know, captured the feeling on September 14, when Montcalm was buried:

[*September 14, 1759 – Friday*]

Charles Michel de Langlade was a member of the melancholy procession of about a hundred people who moved in the gloomy quiet of early evening through the rubble-filled streets to the chapel of the Ursuline Convent. At the head of the line were six young officers of the Quebec garrison and they were carrying on their shoulders a very crudely nailed-together rectangular box.

Within the box was Louis Montcalm.

The general had died at four o'clock this morning, only a few hours after the final rites had been administered by Bishop Pontbriand. Because of the confusion raging inside and out of the city, no carpenter could be located to build a decent coffin and so a faithful old servant of the Ursuline nuns—an individual named Old Man Michael—found a few broken boards which he managed to nail together to form the rough box.

Following closely behind the pallbearers was the Chevalier Ramesay and many of his officers from the Quebec garrison. Behind them came a number of inhabitants of the city—mostly weeping women—plus a dozen or so *coureurs de bois*, including Langlade, and perhaps as many more colony troops.

The Ursuline Convent Chapel had been heavily damaged by cannon fire from Wolfe's batteries across the river. One of the shells had smashed through the ceiling and buried itself in the floor before exploding and causing a large crater. A level space had been prepared in the crater and it was here that the rough coffin was placed, under the direction of three priests and three nuns.

As the entire body of onlookers gathered around, a simple quiet service was held by the light of torches. When it was over, most of the women and a great many of the men were sobbing, while some had fallen to their knees and cradled their faces in their hands. It was not only Montcalm who was being buried here; it was New France.

Even as the dry earth and masonry was being scooped back into the hole to cover the ugly box, Charles Langlade slipped out and moved swiftly to the nearest open exit from the city. With that curious loping gait of the *coureur de bois* he seemed almost to flow rather than walk, and in a few moments the bulk of the city disappeared in the darkness behind him.

Half an hour later, approaching so silently that his presence was not even detected until he stepped into the glow of the small fire, Langlade entered the camp of the western Indians. Most of them had gathered here, two miles from the city, uncertain now what they should do.

Pontiac rose to meet Langlade and in the Ottawa tongue the Canadian half-breed told him that Montcalm was dead and had been buried. For the first time in the many years he had known the war chief, Langlade saw Pontiac's features contort with a grief of great depth. The word spread through the camp and the same grief was reflected by many of the others.

After a while Pontiac and several of the other chiefs sat in council with Langlade while the Canadian explained the state of affairs. With the withdrawal of the regulars, militia, and colony troops at Vaudreuil's orders, Quebec was as good as gone and, with Quebec, Montreal and the rest of Canada.

The ornaments in Pontiac's ears and nose bobbed as he shook his head and his expression became ugly. 'I will not accept English control over Canada,' he said. 'I do not think they can take it and if they should take it, I do not think they can hold it. If I am wrong and they do take it, it is *here* they will hold it, not in our country. We will return now to our villages and stand firmly there, and not an Englishman will be let into our country except by our favor. Quebec may be lost to them; Canada may be lost to them. But as long as he breathes, Pontiac will never embrace the English.'[50]

Stationed on the flanks of Wolfe's army until the fall of Montcalm and the retreat of the French army into Quebec, Langlade often in years after, recounted the events of that decisive battle. He mentioned his Menominee comrades; and his friend La Rose delighted to tell of Langlade's intrepidity and coolness, when in the midst of conflict he would stop to light his pipe. After the battle he was among those who thought Quebec might be defended, and upon its capitulation left for his western home with a sad heart.[51]

❧ *Aftermath*

1760-1800

After the fall of Quebec in September of 1759, Charles Langlade and his Indians returned to the Great Lakes and remained until 1760 when they returned once more to help fight the English.

As the approaching onslaught of three British armies descended upon Montreal in 1760, Langlade, now a lieutenant, was ordered to leave and return to Michilimackinac, where he commanded until the British arrived in September of 1761.

Like many residents of Michilimackinac, Langlade appears to have adjusted to British rule with little difficulty. When in 1763 he heard rumors of an Ojibwa uprising he warned the commandant, George Etherington, of the plot. Etherington, however, did not listen, and the Ojibwas under Madjeckewiss seized the fort. Langlade, at great risk to his own life, rescued Etherington and William Leslye from the stake where they were to be sacrificed.[52]

Langlade later moved to La Baye, where his father was still living, and continued his life as a trader. Here he stayed until the outbreak of the American Revolution, when he was again called to service, this time for England! After bringing Indians to help in the defense of Montreal in 1776, he returned in 1777 with his old comrade in arms, partisan leader Saint-Luc de La Corne, and both served under General John Burgoyne in his campaign.

After the American Revolution ended, Langlade continued to serve in the Indian department as a superintendent. He received a life annuity of eight hundred dollars and a grant of 3000 acres of land in the province of Ontario for his service to the crown.[53]

Langlade remained active in his role as a fur trader and interpreter, until his death, and enjoyed telling about the 99 battles in which he had participated. A companion, recalling Langlade's actions said he "Never saw so perfectly cool and fearless a man on the field of battle."[54]

Notes to Chapter Three

1 Kellogg, p. 315

2 Ibid, p. 315

3 *Collections of the State Historical Society of Wisconsin* (hereafter cited as *WHC*), pp. 3, 199.

4 Ibid

5 Moore, p. 224

6 Kellogg, p. 413

7 Ibid, pp. 418-419

8 Ibid, p. 420

9 Ibid, p. 421

10 Slocum, pp 99-100

11 Rutledge, p. 358

12 Anderson, pp. 28-29

13 Kellogg, p. 422

14 *Dictionary of Canadian Biography* (hereafter cited as *DCB*), p. 431

15 Chartrand, p. 195

16 Anderson, pp 45-46

17 Bird, p. 13

18 O'Meara, pp. 50-52

19 Anderson, pp 46-49

20 *DCB*, p. 400

21 Kopperman, p. 50

22 Hamilton, p. 156

23 Anderson, p. 99

24 Kopperman, p. 52

25 Burnham and Martin, p. 98

26 *DCB*, Vol. IV, p. 563

27 Montcalm's Journal, vol. 7, p. 145

28 Gallup and Shaffer, p. 216

29 Loescher, *The History of Rogers Rangers: Volume 1, The Beginnings* (hereafter cited as *Volume 1*), pp. 111-112

30 Parkman, pp. 307-308

31 Gallup and Shaffer, p. 219

[32] Bearor, *French and Indian War Battlesites: A Controversy* (hereafter cited as *Controversy*), pp. 5-7

[33] Bougainville, p. 81

[34] Loescher, *Volume 1*, p. 123; Bearor, *Controversy*, pp. 45-46

[35] Loescher, *Volume 1*, p. 340

[36] Bird, p. 142

[37] Loescher, *Volume 1*, p. 346; Bougainville, p. 81

[38] Bougainville, p. 81

[39] Cuneo, p. 50

[40] See Brown's Journal excerpts in Bearor, *Controversy*, pp. 11-14

[41] Hamilton, p. 196

[42] Bougainville, p. 95

[43] Bougainville, pp. 135-136

[44] Bougainville, p. 142

[45] Bougainville, p. 143

[46] Bougainville, pp. 135-136

[47] *DCB*, Vol. IV, pp. 563-564

[48] Donaldson, pp 134-135

[49] Eckert, p. 594

[50] Eckert, pp 600-601

[51] Kellogg, p. 435

[52] *DCB*, Vol. IV, p. 564

[53] Zipperer, p. 9

[54] *DCB*, Vol. IV, p. 564

❧ BIBLIOGRAPHY

Anderson, Fred. *Crucible of War*. New York: Alfred E. Knopf, 2000

Bearor, Bob. *The Battle on Snowshoes*. Bowie, Maryland: Heritage Books, Inc., 1997

____. *French and Indian War Battlesites: A Controversy*. Bowie, Maryland: Heritage Books, Inc., 2000

Bird, Harrison. *Battle for a Continent: The French and Indian War, 1754-1763*. New York: Oxford University Press, 1965

Bougainville, Louis Antoine de. *Adventure in the Wilderness: The American Journals of Louis Antoine de Bougainville, 1756-1760*. Edward P. Hamilton, translator and editor. Norman: University of Oklahoma Press

Bourlamaque, Francois Charles de. *Lettres de M. de Bourlamaque au Chevalier de Levis*. Quebec, Canada: Demers & Frere, 1891

Burnham, Koert DuBois and David Kendall Martin. *La Corne St. Luc – His Flame*. Keeseville, New York: Northern New York American-Canadian Genealogical Society, 1991

Charlevoix, Rev P.F.X. *History and General Description of New France*. New York: John Gilmary Shea, 1870

Chartrand, Rene. *Canadian Military Heritage*. Volume I. Montreal: Art Global, Inc. 1993

Collections of the State Historical Society of Wisconsin (WHC).

Costain, Thomas B. *The White and the Gold.* New York: Doubleday and Co., 1954

Cuneo, *Robert Rogers of the Rangers.* Ticonderoga, NY: Fort Ticonderoga Museum, 1988

Day, Gordon. "Rogers' Raid in Indian Tradition." *Historical New Hampshire*, 1982.

Dictionary of Canadian Biography (DCB). 15 vols. Toronto: University of Toronto Press, 1966-1991

Donaldson, Gordon. *Battle for a Continent: Quebec 1759.* Garden City, N.Y.: Doubleday and Co., 1973

Eckert, Allan. *Wilderness Empire.* Little, Brown and Company, 1969.

Gallup, Andrew and Donald Shaffer. *La Marine: The French Colonial Soldier in Canada, 1745-1761.* Bowie, Maryland: Heritage Books, Inc., 1992

Hagerty, Gilbert. *Massacre at Fort Bull: The DeLery Expedition Against the Oneida Carry, 1756.* Providence, R.I.: Mowbray co., 1971

Hamilton, Edward P. *The French and Indian War.* Garden City, N.Y.: Doubleday and Co., 1962

Kellogg, Louise Phelps. *The French Regime in Wisconsin and the Northwest.* Madison: State Historical Society of Wisconsin, 1925; Bowie, Maryland: Heritage Books, Inc., 2001 (reprint)

Kopperman, Paul E. *Braddock at the Monongahela.* Pittsburgh: University of Pittsburgh Press, 1977

Lewis, Meriwether L. *Montcalm, the Marvelous Marquis.* Vantage Press, Inc., 1961

Loescher, Burt G. *The History of Rogers' Rangers: Volume 1, The Beginnings.* San Francisco: self-published, 1946; Bowie, Maryland: Heritage Books, Inc., 2001 (reprint)

Loescher, Burt G. *Genesis: Rogers' Rangers, The First Green Berets.* San Mateo, California: self-published, 1969. Bowie, Maryland: Heritage Books, Inc., 2000, (reprint)

Lucier, Armand Francis. *French and Indian War Notices Abstracted from Colonial Newspapers. Volume 3: January 1, 1758-September 17, 1759.* Bowie, Maryland: Heritage Books, Inc., 2000

Moore, Charles. *The Northwest Under Three Flags, 1635-1796.* New York and London: Harper & Brothers Publishers, 1900; Bowie, Maryland: Heritage Books, Inc., 1989, 2000 (reprint)

O'Callaghan, E.B., ed. *Documents Relating to the Colonial History of the State of New York.* 15 vols. Albany: Weed and Parsons, 1858

O'Meara, Walter. *Guns at the Forks.* Englewood Cliffs, New Jersey: Prentice Hall, Inc., 1965

Parkman, Francis. *Montcalm and Wolfe.* New York: Collier Books, 1962.

Rutledge, Joseph L. *Century of Conflict.* New York: Doubleday, 1956

Slocum, Charles Elihu. *History of the Maumee River Basin from the Earliest Account to its Organization into Counties.* Defiance, Ohio: self-published, 1905; Bowie, Maryland: Heritage Books, Inc., 1997 (reprint)

Steele, Ian K. *Betrayals: Fort William Henry and "The Massacre."* New York: Oxford University Press, 1990

Zipperer, Sandra J. "Sieur Charles-Michel de Langlade, Lost Cause, Lost Culture." *Voyager, Historical Review of Brown County and Northeast Wisconsin,* Winter/Spring, 1999

✤ INDEX

Bob and Holly Bearor at the ceremony for the reburial of the remains of the Marquis de Montcalm, October, 2001.

About the Author

Veteran Heritage Books author Bob Bearor received the venerable Croix de St. Louis from his fellow reenactors in recognition of his outstanding contributions to the field of living history. An expert in 18th-century woods warfare and survival techniques, he served as a consultant to the BBC production, "Ray Mears' Extreme Survival" which featured Rogers' Rangers and the St. Francis Raid. He is the author of *The Battle on Snowshoes* and *French and Indian War Battlesites: A Controversy.* ⚜

OTHER BOOKS BY BOB BEAROR